D0821835

STANFORD LIBRARIES

The Jackson E. Reynolds Book Fund

The Social Democratic Image of Society

By the same author:

Pressure Groups and Political Culture (1967)
Politics and Social Insight (1971)

The Social Democratic Image of Society

A study of the achievements and origins of Scandinavian
Social Democracy in comparative perspective

Francis G. Castles

Routledge & Kegan Paul

London, Henley and Boston

First published in 1978
by Routledge & Kegan Paul Ltd
39 Store Street,
London WC1E 7DD,
Broadway House,
Newtown Road,
Henley-on-Thames,
Oxon RG9 1EN and
9 Park Street,
Boston, Mass. 02108, USA
Set in Journal 10/11 by
Hope Services, Wantage
and printed in Great Britain by
Lowe & Brydone Printers Ltd.
Thetford, Norfolk
© Francis G. Castles, 1978
No part of this book may be reproduced in
any form without permission from the
publisher, except for the quotation of brief
passages in criticism

ISBN 0 7100 8870 1

British Library Cataloguing in Publication Data

Castles, Francis Geoffrey

The social democratic image of society.
1. Socialist parties — Scandinavia
I. Title
329.9'485   JN7066   78-40294

ISBN 0 7100 8870 1

to Heinz and Fay

Contents

Preface

One of the grand paradoxes of politics in the era of industrialism and universal suffrage has been the relatively poor showing of political parties espousing working-class interests. This is hardly the result that would have been expected from a reading of the heated political debates on the extension of the franchise which occurred in most of the Western European nations in the late nineteenth or early twentieth centuries. To give the working man the vote was to give him political power. That is why the defenders of inherited privilege fought against the extension of democratic rights, and it is why the leaders of the embryonic labour movements co-operated so avidly with the liberal forces of reform. Even the earlier socialist ideologues, who had advocated the revolutionary seizure of power by the industrial working class, had not based their prescription on the ineffectiveness of universal suffrage, but on the inherent unlikeliness that the ruling class would be willing to encompass its own self-destruction. In discussing the Chartist demand for the vote, Karl Marx argued that in countries like England, 'where the proletariat forms a large majority of the population' and where 'it has gained a clear consciousness of its position as a class', the inevitable result of universal suffrage would be 'the political supremacy of the working class' (Marx, 1852).

Yet neither in England nor in any of the major countries of Western Europe has the growth of the industrial working class or the extension of democratic participation led to consistent victories for parties which profess working-class aims. Irrespective of their political complexion—

Socialist, Communist, Social Democratic or Labour—such parties have never become the normal parties of government. In some countries, working-class parties have won dramatic political majorities (Britain in 1945 and 1966) only to lose them again in subsequent elections; in others, they have been condemned to political sterility by their encapsulation in coalitions of the Centre (the French Socialists during the Fourth Republic); and, in yet others, they have been permanently excluded from office (the Italian Communist Party since the Second World War). Only in Scandinavia has the picture been substantially different. In Denmark, Norway and Sweden, the Social Democratic parties have, throughout the last half-century, polled a higher percentage of the vote than any other single party. Moreover, the margin by which they have outdistanced their competitors has generally been so considerable as to warrant their description as *dominant parties* (Duverger, 1960, p. 44). Social Democratic electoral strength has been readily transformed into political power and, since the 1930s, the working-class parties of Scandinavia can be distinguished from similar parties elsewhere by their status as natural parties of government.

This book endeavours to explain the political dominance of the Scandinavian Social Democratic parties and to demonstrate the consequences of that dominance. Clearly, both objectives involve the adoption of an explicitly comparative approach. In effect, the explanation of the distinctiveness of the Scandinavian political experience entails showing the relevant circumstances which Denmark, Norway and Sweden have in common and which are not shared by other nations. There is no inherent limitation to the circumstances which might be relevant, and at a minimum it will be necessary to discuss the social bases of party support, the nature of the party systems, the ideological and programmatic appeals of the various parties, and the historical context of political development which has shaped and structured political cleavages and ideas — topics central to the study of comparative political sociology.

The effort to demonstrate the consequences of Social Democratic political dominance in Scandinavia is rather less easy to categorise in academic terms, but, presumably, in so far as it involves charting the impact of political action on social structures and beliefs, it falls somewhere in the area of social policy studies. Comparison is the essence of such an effort. Democratic socialist parties have always maintained that they are the instrumentality of working-class demands and, since only in Scandinavia have such parties been the normal parties of government, it seems natural to ask whether Social Democratic ascendancy has led to greater gains for the working classes of Scandinavia than elsewhere. To answer such a question requires a comparison of policy outcomes in the more economically advanced Western nations, and an examination of the extent to which differences are attributable to the initiatives of democratic socialist governments.

In attempting such a comparison, I intend to adopt as empirical and pragmatic a stance as possible in the hope that I can avoid the fate that my conclusions are dismissed as mere socialist polemic. Indeed, this is not a book about socialism and socialist theory as such, and I will readily concede that if one defines that ideology exclusively in terms of the common ownership of the means of production, then few, if any, of the parties I call 'democratic socialist' (basically the members of the Socialist International) have any rightful claim to that designation. The problem is that there is sometimes a tendency for socialist intellectuals to compare ideals and reality and to find the latter wanting, whereas my objective is to discover whether some aspects of reality are more wanting than others. That seems to me to emerge most clearly by comparing the position of the working class in different nations in terms of empirical indices of income distribution, health care, equality of educational opportunity and the like.

Nevertheless, it would be utterly naive to believe that a discussion of the achievements and origins of the Scandinavian Social Democratic parties, however empirical and pragmatic, could ever be considered as politically uncontroversial. Ever since Marquis Childs described Sweden as *The Middle Way* between capitalism and communism, the Scandinavian experience has been seen as a test case for a particular strategy of democratic socialism (Childs, 1936). This strategy was further elaborated by Anthony Crosland's *The Future of Socialism* (Crosland, 1956). In it he argued not only that of all contemporary societies Sweden came nearest 'the socialist's ideal of the "good" society', but also that the Scandinavian Social Democratic parties' programmatic appeal, which combined advanced welfare and egalitarian policies with a disemphasis on outdated and potentially undemocratic dogmas about state ownership of the means of production, was the recipe for electoral success on the part of democratic socialist parties elsewhere. This reformist interpretation of the Scandinavian experience was influential in shaping the moderate and technocratic stance of the British Labour governments of the 1960s. However, in the wake of the Labour defeat of 1970 a new radical interpretation gained currency. It was suggested that Social Democrats, whether in Scandinavia or elsewhere in Europe, 'have committed themselves to a political system which gives rights to the dominant class to prevent wherever possible the redistribution of class advantages', and that 'this commitment has proved to be at the expense of traditional socialist goals and principles relating to equality' (Parkin, 1971, p. 184). This type of interpretation of the Social Democratic experience has been an influential factor in the leftward shift within the Labour Party during the 1970s.

Clearly then, the extent of Scandinavian Social Democracy's achievement and the reasons for its electoral success are inherently controversial since they touch on vital issues separating Right and Left wings of the European democratic socialist parties. The reformist interpretation points to the achievements of the Scandinavian parties, and, in locating the causes of their electoral success in a specific programmatic appeal, suggests that the Scandinavian experience is replicable elsewhere. The radical interpretation denies the Social Democrats any genuine achievement, and presumably regards their continued electoral success as a basically unimportant historical anomaly. It is the contention of this book that both interpretations are fundamentally incorrect. In chapter 2, I shall attempt to demonstrate that the Scandinavian countries display a significantly higher level of social welfare and a greater concern for the pursuit of egalitarian reform than is typical of other advanced societies, and in chapter 3 I shall discuss the structural and historical circumstances which differentiate their political development, and which make generalisations from the Scandinavian experience inappropriate. It would be too sanguine to hope that this book will make the discussion of Scandinavian Social Democracy any less controversial, but it is my hope that it will make the controversy more informed.

There is a final point which should be stressed. In what I have written above, Scandinavia has been treated almost as if it were a single political entity rather than a grouping of three different countries with separate historical, cultural and political traditions. Such an emphasis must be seen as a consequence of the particular comparison I am attempting to make between countries in which democratic socialist parties have been dominant and those in which they have not, rather than as a general comment on the similarity of the Scandinavian countries. In fact, there are two sorts of scholars in the Scandinavian field: those who seek to compare one Scandinavian country with another and those who attempt to contrast Scandinavia with the rest of the world. Not surprisingly, the first tend to be Scandinavian nationals, 'insiders', whose major reference point is the national peculiarities of their own country, whilst the second tend to be non-Scandinavians, 'outsiders', who wish to use Scandinavia 'as a whole' as a positive or negative reference group to political activity elsewhere. There is no obvious reason why these approaches should be contradictory, and every hope that they might be complementary, once it is realised that they differ less in their depiction of reality than in the perspective from which it is viewed. As its sub-title and preface indicate, this is an 'outsiders' book, but it will rapidly become evident that the first essential of an understanding of what distinguishes the Scandinavian democratic socialist parties from those elsewhere in Europe is an awareness of the differences as well as the similarities existing between the Scandinavian countries. It is, after all, inherent in the logic of comparative analysis that, in order to isolate the common circumstances which cause a given phenomenon, we must be able to distinguish what is common from what is not.

It would also be unfortunate if this essay failed to make clear the rich diversity of political life which characterises the Scandinavian countries, since it would reflect poorly on my capacity to benefit from the knowledge and advice so kindly provided by scholars, politicians and officials in each of these countries. The names of those who have helped me in various ways are too numerous for separate mention. Two individuals, however, deserve my special gratitude. Professor Olof Ruin made it possible for me to visit the Department of Politics, University of Stockholm, during the latter part of 1972, and it was during that period that I first became fascinated by the singularity of Scandinavian political development. Similarly, the kindness of Professor Stein Rokkan has afforded me the opportunity to write this book whilst spending six months as a Visiting Fellow of the Sociology Institute, University of Bergen. It is also appropriate to note with appreciation the financial assistance given me by the Open University, the Swedish Institute and the Nuffield Foundation, which has made possible my travel and research in Scandinavia during the last six years. Last, but by no means least, I wish to thank Rosie Seymour, who helped to provide the moral and grammatical support necessary to write this book.

FRANCIS CASTLES
University of Bergen

A note on terminology

In any book like this which compares and contrasts a large number of political organisations which have similar traditions, similar objectives and similar names there is a real risk of confusion. I have consequently adopted a few simple procedural rules, which help to avoid the worst of the problems, although sometimes at the cost of my prose style. As noted in the Preface, the term *democratic socialist party* is generally used of parties which are adherents of the Socialist International. It has, of course, become the fashion for Communist parties in Western Europe to profess that they are democratic also. That is as it may be, but for the sake of clarity it seems sensible to maintain a distinction which, even if it is becoming less relevant today, was crucial during much of the period covered by this book. I have used the expression *Social Democracy* and its adjectival form in a rather strict sense, since it has in recent times become rather more controversial that it once was. With the single exception of the Norwegian Labour Party, it is used only of parties which use it in self-designation. I claim extenuating circumstances in the case of Norway on the grounds that this book could hardly have been written without a collective noun for the Scandinavian democratic socialist parties, and because I know that *today* the Norwegian Party does not regard the term Social Democracy in an invidious light. Finally, I should mention that I frequently use the expression *bourgeois parties* to refer to the Scandinavian non-socialist parties. This is not a product of any profound analysis of the class composition of these parties, but is merely a reflection of normal Scandinavian usage.

Part one:

Achievements

To toil for others' gain as long as he bears up, to be thrown into wretchedness in old age and die in beggary, such are the laurels which are to inspire the working man to love of his country.

(Anders Chydenius, eighteenth-century Swedish radical cited by Kurt Samuelsson, 1968, p. 122).

The conclusion is irresistible. Sweden, with even less public ownership than ourselves, has succeeded in realising a relatively fair balance between social goods and individual ones. A capitalist economy *can*, it appears, be directed towards different targets from those we are being driven willy-nilly towards here. Swedish Social-Democratic governments have been able to yoke a privately-owned industry to the service of at least those immediate needs of community to which British capitalism has remained impervious to this day.

(Perry Anderson, 1961, p.8).

1
The political dominance of Social Democracy

There was a story current in Swedish political circles in the months
following the defeat of the Social Democrats in the elections of September 1976 that one of the leaders of a party in the new bourgeois coalition had immediately sent out for all the copies of a well-known textbook
on Swedish public administration to be found in the Stockholm book-
shops. Whether apocryphal or not, the story does manage to capture
something of the extraordinary quality of the Swedish Social Democrats'
hold on political office. If the non-socialist leaders needed to turn to
academic experts to understand how the governmental system worked,
it was hardly surprising. The last time those parties had experienced the
tasks of government was at the invitation of the Social Democrats as
part of a wartime National Coalition. Before that the previous exclusively non-socialist government had been a minority Agrarian Party
caretaker administration in the parliamentary recess in the summer of
1936. It is usual to date the advent of Swedish Social Democratic dominance from 1932, and this being so no one who was below pensionable
age in 1976 could previously have voted for a victorious bourgeois
majority government.

There was not a little *Schadenfreude* in the reactions of some of
Western Europe's democratic socialist leaders to the Swedish Social
Democrats' discomfiture. François Mitterand struck an appropriately
ambivalent note when, in an article in *Dagens Nyheter,* he expressed his
surprise that the Swedish Party 'had not accomplished the social appro-
priation of the major means of production, which would have deprived

the private monopolies and cartels of the power to check its socialist aims.' Naturally, the defeat of any working-class party was a disappointment, but to some extent at least it was a consequence of the reformist strategy adopted over four decades of Social Democratic rule. The reactions of the European Right were much more unequivocal. The leadership of the German Christian Democratic Party wrongly read the Social Democratic defeat in Sweden as a portent of imminent victory in the coming Federal election. Margaret Thatcher argued that the end of the Social Democratic era in Sweden was a sign that European socialism's expansionary phase was over. The Social Democratic stranglehold in Scandinavia had been loosened by non-socialist victories in Norway and Denmark in the 1960s, and now, finally, it had relinquished its grasp in its last citadel, Sweden.

There is some element of exaggeration and wish-fulfilment in the more dramatic Right-wing interpretations of the demise of Scandinavian Social Democracy. It should be remembered that at the time of the Swedish election defeat there were minority Social Democratic governments in power in both Denmark and Norway, and that, in fact, the actual decline in the Swedish Party's share of the total vote was less than 1 per cent. Nevertheless, the last decade does seem to have marked a real change in the position of the Scandinavian Social Democratic parties. They may still be the dominant parties in the sense of being substantially larger than their competitors; they may still be the natural parties of government, but they are no longer — as they were in Sweden and Norway, but never in Denmark — the only parties of government. Whether this change of political status is the beginning of a permanent eclipse or merely in the nature of a temporary adjustment is a question which will be touched upon at various points throughout this book. The very fact of the change, however, focuses our attention on the four or five preceding decades of Social Democratic ascendancy.

The most important aspects of that ascendancy have been the continued capacity to hold office and the ability to transform governmental status into programmes of reform. In this chapter, I shall attempt to describe the nature and magnitude of the basic contrasts in the electoral situations of the European democratic socialist parties, which have made it possible for some to be so much more successful than others in these respects. In addition, I shall sketch the various stages of development through which each of the Scandinavian labour movements has acquired and maintained its political ascendancy. Here the objective is partly to uncover similarities rather more subtle than those revealed by the electoral data, and partly to demonstrate the significant differences between the movements. Throughout, the intention is less to offer anything which could properly be called an explanation than to present the main features of the phenomenon whose causes and consequences it will be my task to investigate in subsequent chapters.

1.1 The relative strength of the European Social Democratic parties

Seemingly, the most obvious determinant of a position of political ascendancy within a democratic system will be the size of a party's electoral support. It is, of course, quite possible for a party to have a crucial role in coalition-building whilst only obtaining a rather small share of votes and parliamentary mandates. A strategic position near the centre of the political spectrum can provide a role in government quite out of proportion to size. Such a role has been a not infrequent fate of democratic socialist parties caught between the extremes of Right and Left in many of the European countries this century. However, unless electoral and parliamentary support is of certain minimum dimensions, such a strategic position cannot in the nature of things provide the basis for the enactment of a substantial programme of social reform benefiting the working class. Such was the reality revealed by the almost continuous participation in government of the French Socialist Party throughout the Fourth Republic and the failure of the 'opening to the Left' in Italy in the 1960s. Irrespective of the intentions of party supporters and leaders, the French and Italian democratic socialists were forced by their parliamentary situation to participate in the preservation of the 'immobilist' system and the defence of the status quo.

On purely *a priori* grounds, it seems reasonable to suggest that a democratic socialist party's parliamentary support must be in excess of 25 per cent if it is to be the most consequential influence within a majority coalition government. Unless that level is achieved, whatever programme of reform is offered by the democratic socialists is likely to face not only a hostile majority in parliament as a whole, but also within the governing majority itself. Although, in logic, a smaller percentage of parliamentary support is required to offer the possibility of being the dominant influence within a minority administration, this is offset by the fact that reform initiatives are intrinsically unlikely to succeed against the vast body of parliamentary opinion. As we shall see, in discussing the Scandinavian Social Democrats, and particularly the Danish Party, minority governments can be effective instruments of reform. However, this can only occur when the democratic socialist party in question is one of the largest in the system and at least one of the opposition parties has an ideological or strategic reason for preferring it to its rivals. In Table 1.1, I present a comparison of those European democratic socialist parties whose percentage of parliamentary support has exceeded 25 per cent in at least one election in the five decades between

Table 1.1 Average percentage of democratic socialist vote (by decade)

Countries/ Parties	1920s	1930s	1940s	1950s	1960s
Austria Social Democrats/ Socialist Party	39	41*	42	43	43
Belgium Workers Party/ Socialist Party	37	33	31	36	31
Denmark Social Democrats	35	44	39	40	39
Finland Social Democrats	27	38	26	25	23
France Socialist Party†	28	20	21	15	18
Germany Social Democrats	24	21	29*	30	39
Luxembourg Socialist Party	41††	28	31	37	35
Netherlands Social Democratic Workers/Labour Party	22	22	27	31	26
Norway Labour Party	26	38	43	48	46
Sweden Social Democrats	36	44	49	46	48
Switzerland Social Democrats	26	28	27	27	25
United Kingdom Labour Party	33	34	48*	46	46

Source: all data calculated from Mackie and Rose, 1974.
  *Only one national election in relevant decade.
  †Where the French Socialists entered into electoral alliances with other parties—the Radical Socialists and Socialist Republicans—all the votes have been attributed to the former. This greatly exaggerates the figure for the 1920s.
  ††There are no available election statistics for the early 1920s. The figure cited is for the election of 1928.

1920 and 1969. In fact, this criterion excludes only the Icelandic, Irish and Italian parties, none of which has played any conspicuous role in the recent history of European socialism. I want to emphasise that although the criterion for inclusion is the level of parliamentary support, the data presented are decade by decade averages of the percentage vote. This is necessary since otherwise the peculiarities of the different electoral systems would vitiate the comparison of differential support for the democratic socialist parties in the European countries.

Two important conclusions emerge from an examination of the data in Table 1.1. The first is the absence in most cases of any significant developmental tendency. The majority of the parties seem to have found their natural plateau of electoral support by the 1930s, and only in Norway, the United Kingdom and the Federal Republic of Germany do there appear to have been further appreciable inroads into the non-socialist electorate. This general impression of stable support is reinforced by the demonstrably anomalous character of Finland's electoral situation in the 1930s, and the absence of full data for Luxembourg in the 1920s. The growth of the Finnish Social Democrats in the 1930s was a direct consequence of the suppression of the Communist Party, and the transfer of votes which resulted was reversed in the postwar period. The Luxembourg figure is for a single election in 1928, and the data are unavailable for the previous elections in 1922 and 1925. Since the Socialist Party received only 19.3 per cent of the vote in 1919, the presumption must be that a true average for the 1920s would be somewhat lower.

Since the end of the 1960s, there have been some further significant changes in the level of electoral support for the democratic socialist parties. The German Social Democratic Party has continued its growth, and has polled an average of 44.3 per cent in the elections of 1972 and 1976. The Austrian Socialist Party has finally transcended its traditional boundaries, and in 1971 became only the fourth socialist party in history to win an absolute majority of the votes cast in a free election.[1] Finally, the Danish Social Democrats suffered an extremely severe reverse in the election of 1973, but have, as we shall have occasion to discuss subsequently, retained their pivotal political position, and, in the latest election of February 1977, have recovered virtually all their lost ground. Although the 1970s may mark the emergence of changing patterns of democratic socialist support, the experience of the previous five decades, as revealed in Table 1.1, suggests that the party systems, which had crystallised in the 1920s with the emergence of rival candidates for the working-class vote (Lipset and Rokkan, 1967, p. 50), had already for the most part stabilised by the 1930s in terms of the democratic socialist parties' share of the vote.

This has important implications for what follows. It suggests that whatever the immediate causes of electoral victories and defeats, and however important the choice of strategic options for the maintenance of power, the fundamental causes of a party's relative position must be sought in the particular nature and context of its development. That, in turn, suggests that any facile arguments for the electoral dividends to be expected from the importation of programmes fashioned in other political circumstances should be viewed with the gravest suspicion. There is, indeed, much to be said for Marx's view that whilst 'men make their own history, they do not make it just as they please; they do not make it under circumstances chosen by themselves, but under circumstances directly encountered, given and transmitted from the past' (McLellan, 1975, p. 43).

A second conclusion emerges in respect of the relative size of the various parties surveyed in Table 1.1. In effect, there appear to be two types of party looked at in these terms. If the single anomaly of Luxembourg in the 1920s is ignored, there is a clear divide between parties which have been capable of sustaining their electoral support at or around the 40 per cent level for considerable periods of time and those which have not. In the five decades from 1920 onward, the Austrian, Danish, Norwegian, Swedish and United Kingdom parties fall into the former category, whilst the remaining democratic socialist parties of Western Europe fall into the latter. The 40 per cent level has a greater significance than as an arbitrary point on a continuous scale. Whereas 25 per cent is the minimum level for a real influence within a governmental coalition, the 40 per cent level, under normal circumstances, is the minimum level at which a party can be effectively the pre-eminent force within the political system as a whole. Anything more than the support of one-third of the parliamentary mandates guarantees a party second place in the party competition, but anything more than 40 per cent offers a real chance of majority or unchallenged minority rule.

That 40 rather than 50 per cent is the crucial divide is a consequence of the lack of proportionality of some electoral systems, and the fact that in others the leading party can rely on the tacit or explicit support of a minor party. Non-proportionality has played an important role in democratic socialist victories in Norway and Britain, whilst the tacit support of a variety of different parties in Denmark, have given the Social Democratic parties in these countries the possibility of periods of long and continuous political rule. Obviously, 40 per cent should not be regarded as some magically effective formula. Where neither the advantages of non-proportionality or minor party alliances accrued to the benefit of the Austrian Socialist Party, it had to wait for an absolute majority of the electoral vote to be certain of parliamentary dominance. On the other hand, the empirical relevance of the 40 per cent level is amply illustrated by the assumption of office by Germany's first post-Second World War Social Democratic Chancellor in 1969. It was in that year, that the Party broke through the 40 per cent barrier which had hindered its progress for so long.[2]

The 40 per cent level of support offers a real potential for converting electoral popularity into majority or unchallenged minority rule, but does not by itself provide an adequate criterion for specifying the circumstances under which that potentiality will be actualised. If the five parties which have consistently scored at or around the 40 per cent level are compared in terms of the extent of their participation and status in government, it becomes apparent that the size of a democratic socialist party's electoral support does not in itself determine its role in the political system. This is done in Table 1.2, which shows the average vote received by these five parties during the five decades 1920-69, the number of years they have been in office in that period, and their political status when in government. The years of wartime participation in National governments, and, in the Norwegian case, government in exile, have been excluded, although it should be noted that, whereas the British wartime government was based on a Conservative majority in parliament, in each of the Scandinavian countries the Social Democrats were overwhelmingly the largest political party.[3]

Table 1.2 Average vote, years in office and governmental status of the five largest European democratic socialist parties, 1920-69

Country	Average vote*	Years in office	Governmental status
Austria	42.26	20	Junior partner in Proporz
Denmark	38.72	29	Minority government/dominant partner in coalition
Norway	39.12	25	Majority/minority governments
Sweden	43.39	34	Majority/minority/dominant partner in coalition
United Kingdom	40.26	15	Majority/minority governments

*Calculated from Mackie and Rose, 1974.

It would be overly simplistic to use years in office as an absolute measure of political ascendancy, since the governmental status of the various parties has been so different. It would, for instance, be quite wrong to see the Austrian Socialist Party's twenty years of participation in a consociational arrangement with the Peoples Party as offering an opportunity for political influence equivalent to that provided by the British Labour Party's shorter term of office. At no time did the Austrian Socialist Party command a majority over its coalition partner, whereas Labour's twelve years of postwar government were with the support of a majority of the House of Commons. It would be equally wrong to yield to the temptation to relegate the twenty-nine years of office-holding by the Danish Social Democratic Party simply because so much of it had been in coalition with other parties. The need to arrive at accommodations within a coalition government must necessarily impose some restrictions on carrying out a democratic socialist programme, but the degree to which the Danish Party has dominated the governments of which it has been a part is indicated by the fact that it has never had less than a 25 percentage margin of advantage of parliamentary seats over the combined total of its coalition partners. Finally, it would be mistaken to cling to the old-fashioned view that only a two-party system is 'natural', and that, therefore, only majority democratic socialist government counts. This might afford some pleasure to the more ethnocentric Anglo-Saxons, since it would have the counter-intuitive effect of making the British Party more successful than the Swedish, but only at the cost of demonstrating the Norwegian Labour Party's overall supremacy with sixteen years of continuous majority government from 1945-61.

If years in office cannot be automatically regarded as a measure of political ascendancy in the sense of a capacity to enact programmatic reform, they must, however, be seen as a *sine qua non* for such an ascendancy within the context of a democratic political system. For this reason the rather considerable discrepancies in office-holding revealed in Table 1.2 must be seen as constituting a significant indication of the relative political success of the Scandinavian Social Democrats when compared with the British Labour Party and Austrian Socialist Party. In terms of sheer size of electoral support, the contrast between the different parties' ability to stay in office seems inexplicable, but a distinguishing factor is to be found in the number of parties operating in the respective party systems. The British and Austrian democratic socialist parties operate in the context of what are fundamentally two-party systems. Despite their relatively large size in comparison with many other democratic socialist parties in Europe, within their own political systems they normally have taken second place to a larger party of the Right. In contrast, the Scandinavian nations have multi-party systems in which large Social Democratic parties confront fragmented oppositions.

Table 1.3 Average percentage margin of advantage of democratic socialist parties over the next largest party, or margin of disadvantage compared to the largest party

Countries/ Parties	1920s	1930s	1940s	1950s	1960s
Austria Social Democrats/ Socialist Party	−5	+5	−4	0	−4
Belgium Workers Party/ Socialist Party	−1	0	−12	−9	−5
Denmark Social Democrats	+3	+24	+15	+17	+19
Finland Social Democrats	+5	+14	+2	+2	+1
France Socialist Party	−1	−11	−7	−9	−24
Germany Social Democrats	+6	−12	−2	−17	−7
Luxembourg Socialist Party	+2	−14	−10	0	+1
Netherlands Social Democratic Workers/Labour Party	−7	−7	−4	0	−3
Norway Labour Party	−4	+15	+27	+30	+26
Sweden Social Democrats	+9	+23	+30	+23	+32
Switzerland Social Democrats	−2	+4	+5	+2	+2
United Kingdom Labour Party	−8	−2	+11	−1	+3

Source: all data calculated from Mackie and Rose, 1974 (all previous notes to Table 1.1 are relevant here also).

Whereas the labour movements of Britain and Austria have frequently represented a minority political influence, the similarly sized labour movements of Scandinavia have been overwhelmingly the single most important focus of political loyalties in their respective nations. They may remain technically minorities of the population as a whole, but they can be rightfully described as *dominant minorities*.

The use of the concept of a dominant party system, characterized as one in which a particular party consistently outdistances all the others, has recently been criticised for obfuscating 'the systemic properties of the countries it sorts out' (Sartori, 1976, p. 195). There does not appear to be a similar objection to the use of a measure of relative dominance as a means of distinguishing amongst political parties of a particular ideological persuasion. In such a case, the level of dominance characterises the party rather than the system, and may, indeed, be seen as an indication of the effect of different party systems on a particular kind of party. In Table 1.3, we present such a comparison of the relative dominance of the European democratic socialist parties in the five decades 1920-69.

It needs to be stressed that Table 1.3 should be read in conjunction with Table 1.1. It is my contention that both sizes of electoral support and relative dominance within the party system are crucial determinants of a democratic socialist party's potential for transforming governmental status into reform capacity. Thus, although Table 1.3 shows that the Finnish and Swiss Social Democrats have been the largest parties in their respective political systems for many decades, and whilst this has given both an important executive role, it would be mistaken to assume that this role necessarily offered a greater potential for political influence than the twelve years of Labour majority government in Britain in the 1940s and 1960s.

However, precisely because the two tables should be read in conjunction, the ascendancy of the Scandinavian parties emerges with a doubled force. The Danish, Norwegian and Swedish parties have not only been amongst the five largest democratic socialist parties in terms of electoral support during the four decades 1930-69, but also, they have, throughout that period, maintained very considerable margins of advantage over opposing parties. No other European democratic socialist parties have anything like a comparable record of overwhelming victory over their political rivals. Even very large margins of comparative advantage are not a *guarantee* that governmental status will be achieved, as is indicated by the Norwegian Labour Party's defeat in the 1965 election with a margin of political dominance of 22 per cent of the electorate. It is, however, quite apparent that the Scandinavian Social Democratic parties' exceptional record as the natural parties of government since the early 1930s is closely associated with this feature of their performance.[4]

The elaboration of the conditions explaining the unusually high level of relative dominance exhibited by the Scandinavian democratic socialist parties will be the subject of chapter 3. For the moment, it seems reasonable to argue that, together, the size of electoral support and the extent of relative dominance are sufficient criteria to establish the distinctive potential of the Scandinavian Social Democratic parties to have effected reforms benefiting the working class. Whether this potential has been realised is the question that will be investigated in chapter 2. Before discussing that, however, it is necessary to understand something of the stages of development through which each of the Scandinavian Social Democratic parties has acquired and maintained its political ascendancy.

1.2 The emergent Scandinavian labour movements

To look at democratic socialist parties as mere machines for registering a large share of the electoral turnout is a convenient abstraction for contrasting the relative success of different parties, but it becomes quite untenable in developmental perspective. Socialist parties throughout Europe have, from their earliest origins, been closely related to other organisations based on the working-class culture and *milieu*; must obviously trade unions, but also mutual protection societies, co-operatives, temperance associations and workers' educational groups. Together, these organisations have constituted the labour movement. It is the extent to which that movement has been both integrated and united — in terms of organisational links, common policy programmes and objectives, and comradely solidarity — which has been the major determinant of the ability of the industrial working class to transform its crucial role in the social structure of capitalism into an effective voice in politics. The development of the Scandinavian labour movements has, on the whole, been characterised by a high level of integration and unity, but there have been important areas of dissimilarity, and, as will be demonstrated later, these are not unrelated to differences in the movements' political achievements.

Three aspects of the development of the Scandinavian labour movements have been particularly influential in conditioning their strength, unity and integration. These were the relative absence of impediments to working-class industrial and political organisation, the timing and social context of organisational growth, and the nature of the strategic choices faced by the various movements at different times. The extent to which emergent trade unionism and socialism have been subject to state legitimated violence does not permit of exact measurement. It is, moreover, an emotional subject; every labour movement having its martyrs and traditions of oppression. It is quite possible to describe as persecution the authorities' reaction to the Thrane Movement of 1848-51 in Norway, the Lasalle inspired 'International Workers' Association in Denmark' between 1871-7 and the Sundsvall strike in 1876 in Sweden, since in each case some of the leaders were imprisoned for short terms. But compared with Europe as a whole the official response was remarkably mild, and it is at least as significant that the Danish Constitution of 1849 explicitly established the right to form associations without prior permission, and that Thrane's 'workers' union' on the Chartist model was allowed three years of campaigning before its leaders were convicted for sedition. It is possible that the Swedish trade unions and Social Democratic Party faced official opposition until slightly later than elsewhere in Scandinavia, perhaps, because it was in Sweden that the occurrence of industrialisation and democratisation was most tardy, but by the 1890s freedom of industrial and political organisation was the general rule throughout Scandinavia.[5]

Indeed, by that time the respective labour movements had begun to become assimilated to a uniquely Scandinavian institutional development of the latter half of the nineteenth century: the growth of the 'popular movements'. These originally began as cultural and economic expressions of the demand of the peasant majorities in these societies for full integration within their national communities. They included temperance movements, producer co-operatives, movements of dissent within the Established Church and associations for popular enlightenment. They were 'popular' in the sense of representing popular aspirations against the claims of ancient right and established privilege. But, because in Scandinavia there was an extraordinary temporal conjunction of the achievement of a substantial degree of political influence by the peasantry and the emergence of the nascent labour movements, it was difficult to deny the mantle of popular legitimacy to the labour movements also. This was all the more true to the extent that there were cross-cutting affiliations between the movements; with many working-class leaders adhering to the temperance movement as a means of eradicating a social evil which diminished the worker's sense of responsibility to his fellows. Moreover, as the nineteenth century drew to a close, and the peasant proprietors became somewhat more conservative in inclination, the growing campaign for universal suffrage took on something of the character of a popular movement uniting the urban workers and the more progressive elements of the middle class.

Both the relative mildness of the official opposition to the labour movement, and the legitimacy conferred by its role as part of a wider movement for popular rights, meant that the Scandinavian working-class organisations did not develop the alienation and siege-mentality that was a frequent consequence of official repression elsewhere in Europe. In the Scandinavian climate of opinion there was an early tendency toward moderation, well expressed by the unanimous resolution of the constituent congress of the Swedish Social Democratic Party in 1889:

> This congress rejects entirely the occasional insinuations of some of our foes that we, because we are still not fully supported by the people, intend to risk the very existence of the labor movement by a violent upheaval. . . .
>
> This congress realizes that, in comparison with the revolutionary Social Democratic Labor Party which represents the propertyless working class, the bourgeois parties are linked together by reactionary tendencies common to the all. . . . In Sweden, economic conditions are such that this congress would judge it premature to refuse co-operation under all circumstances (Landauer, 1959, p. 438).

This middle course, between an acknowledgement of the principle of class struggle inherited from the German Social Democratic platforms on which the Scandinavian parties each based their programmes, and a denial of its revolutionary implications, was typical of all the parties until at least the turn of the century. So too was the willingness to envisage collaboration with the more progressive elements of the bourgeoisie, which was less a function of 'economic conditions' and more a consequence of a common interest in democratic reform.

The ideological similarity of the Scandinavian Social Democratic parties at this time was by no means a reflection of identical contexts of social and economic development. Social mobilisation, as measured by the percentage of the population living in urban localities and employed in non-agricultural occupations, was considerably higher in Denmark than in her Northern neighbours throughout the nineteenth century (Kuhnle, 1975, pp. 44-8). In terms of a wider comparative perspective, it might be argued that the Danish pattern of industrial development was somewhere intermediate between the early and extremely gradual pace displayed by Britain and the rather late and very rapid growth experienced by Norway and Sweden.[6] In the latter countries, an appreciable class of industrial workers did not appear until the 1880s at the very earliest, whereas in Denmark such a grouping appeared some decades earlier as a consequence of the gradual transformation of the previously existing social formation of urban craftsmen and journeymen.

This divergence between the Scandinavian countries has had important implications for the development of the respective working-class movements. The Danish trade unions grew up in an environment of small-scale production, and were nurtured by the 'organisational propensities' inherited from the guild system which had only finally been dissolved in 1862 (Galenson, 1968, p. 111). Thus, there developed in Denmark a craft structure of small independent unions, which, although they were forced by the solidarity of the employers into a centralised organisation as early as 1898, have always jealously attempted to retain some element of separate identity and initiative in collective bargaining. In Norway and Sweden, trade unions developed in the context of a significantly more modern type of large-scale factory production. The earliest unions were also, quite naturally, based on skilled crafts, but, without any viable tradition of urban guild organisation, there was a strong pull in the direction of industrial unionism, and this was fostered by an unrelenting pressure from the employers' side for industry-wide settlements. The Swedish Federation of Labour, set up in the same year as that in Denmark, had a somewhat greater concentration of authority at the centre and, although for several decades the basic bargaining unit was the industrial union, there was a gradual shift in power to the centre which became decisive by the late 1930s. The Norwegian Federation of Labour was founded in 1899, and from the outset had a level of central authority only rivalled by the Swedish organisation some decades later. These differences in trade union structure have had some impact on the ability of the respective labour movements to achieve mutually acceptable accommodations between unions and government once the Social Democrats assumed power. Moreover, the Danish tradition of craft autonomy has not only caused occasional difficulties in this respect, but has also inhibited wage-levelling initiatives of the kind pursued by the more centralised trade union movements in Sweden and Norway under the slogan of 'the wage policy of solidarity'. It should, however, be emphasised that, whilst these differences are of some importance in understanding the relative strength and unity of the respective Scandinavian labour movements, they are differences in degree rather than in kind. Even the Danish Federation of Labour would be considered highly centralised by contrast with the British TUC (Ingham, 1974, p. 64).

Denmark's earlier industrialisation also led to a somewhat earlier growth of Social Democracy, which traces its origins to the publication of the weekly paper, *Socialisten,* in 1871. The Norwegian Labour Party was founded in 1887 and the Swedish Social Democratic Party some two years later. Despite this difference in timing, the rather high level of integration which seems to have characterised the development of each of the labour movements can be regarded as a consequence of the fact that in their early years the relationships of trade unions and socialist groupings were extremely diffuse. Whilst organisational differentiation emerged with time, there was no intention to create separate institutional identities, much less to assume that one organ of the labour movement would be a mere agency of the other. Knut Heidar's description of the Norwegian reality seems to have a general applicability to the Scandinavian countries:

> The relationship between the two most important sections of the labour movement — party and trade unions — has for most of the time been 'one body, two arms': the separation was much clearer in organisational structure than organisational practice (Heidar, 1977, p. 293).

Of course, there have been some differences in the mechanisms devised to provide integration at various levels within the different organs of the labour movements. Most noticeable has been the absence of any form of collective affiliation in Denmark in contrast with the existence of this linkage at the grass roots level of the union branch in both Norway and Sweden. Since this aspect of the organisation of the Danish Party was settled some two decades before it was decided by the other parties, it seems probable that this too may have been a consequence of early development. This difference does not, however, seem to have been a force retarding the emergence of the Danish Social Democrats as a party of expanding mass membership until just before the Second World War (Svensson, 1974, p. 134). From the 1950s, there has been a serious decline in Danish Social Democracy's capacity to attract active adherents, but this does not seem so much a cause as a symptom of declining support. Certainly, it cannot be readily attributed to the lack of collective membership, since the Norwegian Party manifests precisely the same tendency.[7]

From the time when organisational differentiation first emerged within the labour movements, there have been attempts to create institutional mechanisms with the purpose of ensuring policy co-ordination between party and trade union leaders. In both Sweden and Denmark, the Chairman of LO — in all the Scandinavian countries, the name invariably used for the trade union central organisations — is a member of the Social Democratic Party Executive as of right, whilst, in Norway, there is a special 'co-operation committee' which brings together leading figures in the Labour Party and LO. There have, of course, been occasions when relations have been strained in each of the countries but, in general, harmony has prevailed. Moreover, as will be demonstrated subsequently there was been extensive collaboration in policy initiation and innovation.

The timing and context of social development had several other important effects in separating the experience of the Danish labour movement from those of the other Scandinavian countries. The major contrast between modernisation in Denmark and the countries to the north was not just a question of small-scale versus large-scale industry but of an economy whose important source of wealth was the export of the products of a highly competitive and commercial agriculture compared with economies geared to factory-based production. Although Denmark's class of urban craft workers had a major influence in importing socialist influence into Scandinavia in the latter part of the nineteenth century, and had forced the employers into accepting the world's first voluntary agreement regulating industrial disputes and recognising the equal status of trade unions,[8] by 1900 they probably constituted no greater percentage of the population than their more proletarian brothers in Norway and Sweden (Lafferty, 1971, Table 2.2). It might be argued that the Danish labour movement remained at a higher level of political consciousness as measured by the Social Democratic share of the vote, but by about 1910-2 all three Scandinavian parties were polling approximately 25 per cent. The rates of growth of virtually every indicator of working-class development suggested that it would be Sweden and Norway that now forged ahead as Scandinavia's leading labour movements. While military, political and economic events interfered with the complete fulfilment of such an extrapolation of existing trends for almost two decades, it was the Swedish and Norwegian, but not Danish, parties which successfully negotiated the 30 per cent barrier before the First World War.

In summary, I would argue that the timing and social context of the emergence of the Danish labour movement resulted in a process of development which was earlier, more gradual, and which peaked sooner, but at a somewhat lower level than was the case elsewhere in Scandinavia. The Danish Social Democrats polled their highest vote in 1935 with 46.1 per cent. Thus, in one of the most perfectly proportional electoral systems ever devised, the Party never achieved majority government. In a way this was ironic, since gradual development had been reflected in gradualist policy, and of all the Western European democratic socialist parties, the Danish Social Democrats have been possibly the most consistent advocates of the parliamentary road to a socialism which was to be not merely in the interests of the working class, but of society as a whole. Alastair Thomas offers a concise statement of this ideological stance.

> Although the Social Democratic Party is based firmly on the working-class, it has never seen itself as a narrow class party but has always sought to represent the disadvantaged throughout society. Its concept of Socialism has therefore been a society which itself

controlled the means of production and in which the state acted in the interests of the whole society. A parliamentary majority would allow real social reforms and an end to the worst consequences of capitalism, including unemployment and economic crises, to the benefit not only of labour but of smallholders, small tradesmen and the poor generally (Thomas, 1977, p. 254).

With views of this kind, it is hardly surprising that the political arm of the emergent Danish labour movement saw its immediate strategic objective as the full democratisation of political life.

If it can be argued that Denmark's early and relatively gradual economic development resulted in a labour movement whose major objective was social reform by parliamentary means, it seems reasonable to suppose that the lateness and rapidity of industrial growth in Sweden and Norway might lead to greater labour radicalism in those countries. There is a sense in which this did happen, and the greater influence of large-scale factory production in these latter countries was reflected in party programmes which, until at least the late 1920s, emphasised the crucial importance of the collective ownership of the means of production as the agency of socialist advance to a far greater degree than was the case in Denmark. In another sense, the link between rapid economic development and labour radicalism appears rather less convincing insofar as the major contrast between the Scandinavian labour movements during the two decades from 1910 was the clear parliamentary emphasis manifested not merely by the Danish but also by the Swedish Party, and the Norwegian Party's flirtation with revolutionary ideas and its temporary adherence to the Communist Third International.

These differences in radicalism between the Scandinavian parties—the consistent gradualism of the Danish Party, the greater emphasis on collective ownership in Sweden and Norway, and the revolutionary rhetoric of the Norwegian Party—have generally been accounted for by contemporary political sociologists with the argument that not only was there a major contrast between the rates of development of Denmark and the countries to the North, but also that the rapidity of industrial growth was still greater in Norway than in Sweden. Indeed, the supposed nature of the Scandinavian experience of the relationship between differential rates of economic development and degrees of labour radicalism has been generalised as a widely accepted theory of the destabilising impact of rapid economic growth.[9] Neither as generalised theory, nor as portrayal of Scandinavian development can these views be unequivocally accepted, if only because economic historians provide evidence which suggests that, to the extent that there was a difference in Norway and Sweden's growth rates in the first two decades of this century, it was

Sweden's that was the more rapid (Kuznets, 1971, pp. 38-9). It would be incorrect to assume that the economic context of change was irrelevant to the varying degrees of radicalism displayed by the Scandinavian labour movements, but a considerable part of that difference seems attributable to political rather than economic variables.[10]

It is in the different strategic choices facing the respective labour movements in the early part of this century that one can locate an explanation for the greater inclination to revolutionary activism exhibited in Norway. Paradoxically, this was largely a consequence of the earlier and more complete democratisation of the Norwegian political system. Parliamentarianism was forced on the reluctant Conservatives in 1884, and manhood suffrage was the natural consequence of the major Liberal electoral victory in 1897, only a decade after the foundation of the Norwegian Labour Party. In its early years, the Labour Party collaborated with the Liberals on the suffrage question, and this co-operation carried over to social policy issues in the period leading up to the dissolution of the Union with Sweden in 1905. Thereafter, the Labour Party began to feel that there were no further advantages to be reaped from co-operation with the Liberals, and certain organisational gains to be made by attempting to attract support away from Liberal worker organisations in the cities. Moreover, Labour's disenchantment with its former allies was exacerbated by the realisation that the new and, supposedly, more democratic electoral system which had been adopted in 1905 systematically favoured the Liberals at its expense.[11] The fact that democratisation was formally accomplished made it difficult for the moderates to explain the failure of parliamentary action to procure results in terms of policy reform, whilst the manifest unfairness of the translation of votes into parliamentary mandates made it easy for radicals to focus attention on class warfare as an alternative means of resolving the economic contradictions of capitalist society.

In contrast to this situation in which the Norwegian labour movement became progressively isolated from other social forces, the absence of a comparable degree of democratisation in Denmark or Sweden until well into the second decade of the twentieth century made collaboration a strategic necessity. In Denmark, the Social Democrats were active participants with the Liberals in the prolonged struggle for parliamentarianism, which was finally achieved in 1901. This was victory enough for a large part of the Liberal Party, but a Radical-Liberal faction continued to press for the extension of the suffrage in alliance with the Social Democrats. This was accomplished in 1915 by a Radical-Liberal minority government with Social Democratic support, and in the Danish context it was natural enough for the compliment to be returned in 1924, when a minority Social Democratic administration with a policy of moderate social reform was supported by the Radical-Liberals. In Sweden, the forces resisting democratisation were, if anything, more determined than in Denmark, and the Conservatives were only willing to concede the parliamentary principle at the end of the war after the situation within the army and navy had become 'very revolutionary'.[12]

In the preceding two decades, the demand first for manhood suffrage and then for parliamentary sovereignty had united the Social Democrats and Liberals, and this extended period of parliamentary collaboration was a potent agency for the deradicalisation of a party whose programmatic commitment to revolutionary takeover had always been somewhat suspect. Already by 1914, Tingsten suggests, 'through parliamentary activity in the increasingly democratised state, democracy itself came to be considered not only as a means but as a fundamental principle' (Tingsten, 1973, p. 699).

The nature of the strategic situation facing the different Scandinavian labour movements conditioned their response. The absence of the basic prerequisites of democratic participation in Denmark and Sweden forced the Social Democrats into a prolonged collaboration with the more progressive sections of the bourgeoisie. The nature of the values thus inculcated and, particularly, the idea that the basic socialist reforms to which they were committed were in a sense an extension to the social sphere of liberal political reforms, made it quite impossible for Stauning or Branting, the Danish and Swedish Party leaders, to refuse the opportunity to form Social Democratic administrations in the 1920s to secure those working-class reforms which were so urgently needed. The situation in Norway was quite different; democratic rights had been granted, but the labour movement was no nearer in achieving its goals. In 1919, the Liberals, realising that eventually the growth in the working-class electorate must, with the existing electoral system, lead to their own permanent exclusion from power, introduced a system of proportional representation. It was too late from the point of view of the unity of the Labour Party. This had been taken over by the radical Tranmael faction in 1918, had adhered to the Third International in 1919, and in 1921 lost its moderate wing, which broke away to form a separate Social Democratic Labour Party. In 1923, a majority of the radical wing left Comintern, and within a few years, with the exception of a small Communist faction, the Labour Party was reunited. The first, extremely short-lived, Labour cabinet took office in 1928.

In concluding this discussion of the emergent Scandinavian labour movements, two brief points should be made regarding the Norwegian Party's temporary departure from the parliamentary path to socialism. The first is that the various party splits had very serious implications for the integration of the Norwegian labour movement as a whole.

Previously, the trade unions had been largely content to let the Party leadership exercise primacy in the political field, but now, as the price for providing the initiative and financial backing for reunifying the Party, they obtained a much greater influence in policy-making which, amongst other things, was used to hasten the deradicalisation of the Party. The second point is that the Labour Party's radicalism had singularly little impact outside the realm of ideas. No overt revolutionary action was taken, and the radical wing of the Party left Comintern precisely because it was unwilling to accept the doctrine, imposed from outside, that civil war was the appropriate strategy for Norwegian conditions. Ulf Torgersen suggests that 'non-socialist politicians had fully realized Labour presented no threat at all to the parliamentary system even before 1926 when [it] was reunited after the schism' (Torgersen, 1974, p. 200). Given the labour movement's earliest experience of legitimation as part of the groundswell of democratic popular participation, and the Labour Party's prospects of playing a major governmental role under the new system of proportional representation, it would have been more than surprising if they had presented such a threat.

1.3 The road to power

In each of the Scandinavian countries the 1920s was in a sense a period of interregnum. In each, the fundamental democratic reforms had been accomplished — largely by the Liberals, but, in Denmark and Sweden, with Social Democracy playing an important supporting role. The Conservatives were on the defensive and had little prospect of increasing their share of the vote. The Liberals, with their democratising mission completed, showed a strong tendency to separate into their constituent elements. This process began in Denmark with the emergence of the progressive Radical-Liberal faction in 1905. Given the strong agricultural basis of Danish economic life, it was the traditional Liberal Party which became the representative of the more conservative rural interests, and the Radicals who became the spokesmen for the smallholders in the country and more progressive elements in the towns. With the declining importance of agriculture in Norwegian and Swedish economic life, the basis for division was rather different. The Liberals transformed themselves into parties of social liberalism, whilst that section of their support which had derived primarily from an identification with the economic interests of small- and medium-sized peasant holdings shifted over to newly formed Agrarian parties. In what were, before the Second World War, fundamentally four-party systems, the Social Democratic parties, with their rapidly expanding working-class basis for support, had much the best long-term prospects. In the short-term, however, the

situation was one of parliamentary deadlock in which minority governments could only formulate policy within the constraints imposed by
the veto power of the parliamentary opposition. It was a period which
was unpropitious for extensive social reform, on economic as much as
on parliamentary grounds. Intractable problems of economic stabilisation and unemployment preoccupied administrations of all political
complexions. The Social Democrats were to be distinguished from
other parties by their softer line on such issues as the level of wages for
relief-work and provision of unemployment insurance. It is notable that
the Danish and both the Swedish Social Democratic administrations of
the 1920s fell on unemployment-related measures which involved
a degree of public expenditure which was entirely unacceptable to even
the most progressive elements of non-socialist opinion.

The parliamentary and policy-making impasse of the 1920s was resolved by the emergence of the Social Democrats as the natural parties
of government in the 1930s. Although there are, of course, differences
in the circumstances under which this transition to Social Democratic
rule occurred, what is most striking are the similarities in respect of
electoral strength, ideological transformation and willingness to co-
operate with other parties. By the time the Scandinavian parties began
their extended tenures of office (in Denmark, 1929; in Sweden, 1932,
and in Norway, 1935) each had succeeded in obtaining at least 40 per
cent of the popular vote and a comparable percentage of parliamentary
mandates. This provided no certainty that the Social Democrats would
be able to form a government, as was demonstrated between 1926-8 in
Sweden and 1933-5 in Norway, but for the next three decades a Social
Democratic poll in excess of 40 per cent was a virtual guarantee that
the Party could take office either alone or in coalition.[13] The fragmentation of the opposition into at least three bourgeois parties plus, on
occasions, a number of even smaller parties of both Right and Left, has
made it very difficult to find the necessary cohesion to offer a credible
alternative to Social Democratic rule.

To make such a judgment with the benefit of hindsight is considerably easier than it would have been at the time. Towards the end of the
1920s, it might well have appeared more probable that fundamental
ideological disagreements between socialists and non-socialists, and
closely related divergencies between the working class's practical need
to alleviate the problems of unemployment and the conventional wisdom
of financial orthodoxy, would have provided the basis for a last-ditch
stand by the bourgeois parties. In Denmark, the ideological irreconcila-
bilities were least, and the advent of Social Democratic dominance
appeared as only one further step in the long evolution of partnership
between the Social Democrats and Radical-Liberals. In the absence of

any commitment by the former to large-scale plans for common owner-ship, it was possible to formulate a joint legislative programme for the 1929 election including 'increased action against unemployment, ex-panded opportunity for smallholders to acquire land, the broadening of social legislation, educational reforms, and anti-monopoly laws' (Miller, 1968, p. 38). The two parties also had common interests in constitu-tional revision to abolish the conservative guarantees inherent in the upper house of parliament, the *Landsting*. Moreover, the experience of three years of strict financial orthodoxy by a Liberal administration had undermined public confidence in the sovereign virtues of a balanced budget. In the circumstances of the Great Depression, this attitude, which was a product of pragmatic experience rather than theoretical reflection, stood the government in good stead. Denmark's overwhelm-ingly vulnerable position as an agricultural exporter also had the effect of encouraging both Conservatives and Liberals to countenance measures of government economic intervention that would previously have been anathema. Most significant, perhaps, in long-term perspec-tive, the government's response to an employers' demand made in 1933 for a 20 per cent wage reduction backed by the threat of a lock-out was to legislate a one-year ban on all strikes and lockouts and the continuation of all existing wage agreements. The 'moderate' Danish Social Democrats reaped their reward as the protector of working-class interests in the 1935 election when they polled 46 per cent of the vote, and a year later the permanent Conservative majority in the *Landsting* succumbed to the joint onslaught of the Social Democrats and Radical-Liberals. When in 1939 this alliance once again won an electoral victory in elections to the lower house, the Social Democrats might reasonably claim that for them the 1930s was a testimony to 'the inevitability of gradualism'.

The prospects of the Swedish Social Democrats in the late 1920s were less than propitious. In 1928 they suffered their first major elec-toral reverse in a campaign which focused on the dangers of bolshevism and socialisation which the bourgeois parties argued would be implicit in their victory. The Liberals, although declining rapidly in strength, and divided into pro- and anti- Prohibitionist wings, held the balance of power in parliament, and adhered to a strictly *laissez-faire* economic policy combined with stringent financial orthodoxy. The Agrarian Party had played up the socialist menace in the election, and had benefited from the votes of the rural lower classes, who were persuaded by the view that high industrial wages forced up the prices of the manufactured goods on which the agricultural sector was dependent (Söderpalm, 1975, p. 264). The only real advantage in the situation was that a Social Democratic administration did not have to take responsibility for the disastrous decline in agricultural prices which was the first symptom of imminent economic depression. The joint impact of electoral defeat and the impending collapse of the existing economic structure provided the Social Democratic leadership with the incentive for a fundamental reappraisal of strategy. To do nothing beyond preach the virtues of social ownership and await the inevitable disintegration of the capitalist system was one possibility, but it had the disadvantage of proving the impotence of Social Democracy at the same time as proved the failure of capitalism. A group within the Party led by Ernst Wigforss, and strongly supported by Per Albin Hansson, the future Social Democratic Prime Minister, promoted the alternative of a massive reflationary policy of government-sponsored public works and deficit financing. Inspired by the Stockholm School of economists, which in many ways fore-shadowed Keynesian ideas, such a policy promised not only to resolve the economic crisis, but to establish the Social Democrats unequivo-cally as the party of full employment. Proposals based on the latter strategy were presented in the parliamentary sessions of 1930 onwards, and in the 1932 election the Social Democrats obtained 45 per cent of the parliamentary mandates. However, the Social Democratic minority government which was formed was still confronted by a majority favour-ing the old-fashioned virtues of financial rectitude, and the resulting stalemate was only overcome the following year, when a deal was arranged with the Agrarians whereby they guaranteed their support in return for what amounted to agricultural subsidies. The inherent eco-nomic logic of the crisis measures adopted by the Social Democrats was to substitute public investment for deficient private initiative, but in the process they established the government's role as the primary regulator of the economic mechanism. By the summer of 1936 the total of jobless had declined from 139,000 to 21,000, and the Party obtained 48 per cent of the seats in the lower house. Although for the moment in formal coalition with the Agrarians, the Social Demo-crats had established a position which was unchallenged for four decades.

It is, perhaps, unnecessary to dwell on the details of the Norwegian Party's progress to power, which was somewhat slower than in Denmark and Sweden as befits a parliamentary party which only deleted refer-ences to the 'dictatorship of the proletariat' from its programme after 1927. Again the Great Depression was the catalyst which made the Party abandon its previous beliefs that the only function of a socialist party in a capitalist state was to struggle for the workers' interests whilst attempting to seize power, and that socialist transformation could not begin before that seizure. As Finn Moe noted only a few years after the adoption of a new policy by the Labour Party which won it sweeping gains in the 1933 election:

> In the new policy, these two activities have been merged together. This was the natural result of its analysis of the crisis. It was led to lay stress upon what was formerly considered a reformist activity, the fight against the depression. But its analysis clearly showed that this depression was a crisis in the capitalist system itself and that it could be solved only by reforms in the entire structure of the capitalist society. Thus the fight for the immediate interests of the workers — the fight against the depression — was eventually tied up with the revolutionary task of changing the structure of society (Moe, 1937, pp. 33-4).

Despite the Labour election gains of 1933, the non-socialist parties hung on until a 'Crisis Agreement' between the Labour and Agrarian parties initiated a programme on Swedish lines in 1935: deficit financing, public works, the introduction of social-welfare reforms, and a variety of price support agreements in the agricultural sector. The Norwegian Labour Party, although for many decades thereafter a more ardent protagonist of state regulation than the other democratic socialist parties of Scandinavia had, after the mid-1930s, joined them as a party wholly committed to the achievement of social reform within a parliamentary framework. In 1938, this commitment was given symbolic expression when the one-time member of Comintern declared its formal adherence to the Socialist international.

I have laid some stress on the historical processes by which the Scandinavian Social Democratic parties first achieved dominant political status not merely because of their intrinsic interest, but also because of their wider comparative significance. An important aspect of the Social Democrats' achievement in the 1930s was not only that they attained office at a time when democratic socialism elsewhere remained impotent to protect working-class interests, but also that their programme was of a kind which did not alienate the substantial class of peasant proprietors. In those other countries of Europe which were at a comparable stage of economic development, the implementation of conventional economic doctrine at a time of agricultural crisis was a potent force driving the peasantry into the arms of fascism. Indigenous fascist parties had virtually no significance in Scandinavia, and much of the credit for this must be attributed to the joint willingness of the Social Democrats and the farmers' parties to reach agreements despite initial ideological misgivings on both sides. Furthermore, the success of this collaboration was a precedent for postwar attempts to bring about wide-ranging social reforms by accommodation with other social forces rather than by direct confrontation. As the anti-Depression policy had demonstrated, this did not necessarily mean advancing at the pace of the slowest, but rather of finding means of creatively fashioning majorities of progressive opinion.

The process by which the Social Democratic parties achieved political dominance in the 1930s was also an extremely significant factor in cementing the close integrative ties which bound the Scandinavian labour movements. The achievement of political office by a democratic socialist party necessarily has profound effects on its relationships with the trade unions. In particular, such a party, in assuming administrative responsibility, ceases to be able to regard the potentially disruptive effects of strike activity on the community as just another skirmish in the class war. Therefore, in so far as the unions feel themselves to be part of a unified labour movement, they must accept restraint on their actions in a whole variety of ways. Clearly, their willingness to do so is largely a function of the extent to which they feel that a democratic socialist government can advance their fundamental interests. In this sense, the fact that the whole strategy of the Scandinavian Social Democratic parties centred around the need to guarantee full employment and prevent wage reductions, which were the trade unions' chief demands throughout the interwar period, ensured that the trade unions felt that any restraints that were temporarily demanded of them could be justified in terms of long-term advantages to their members. The contrast between the actions of the Scandinavian Social Democratic parties in power in the 1930s and legacy of mistrust and betrayal left in the wake of the defeat of the British Labour government of 1931 is, perhaps, sufficient explanation of the much greater unity and integration displayed by the Scandinavian labour movements in the postwar years.

1.4 The mechanisms of Social Democratic ascendancy

Immediately after the Second World War, all the Scandinavian labour movements elaborated programmes which, starting from the premise that the major postwar problem would be severe economic recession, advocated the extension of state ownership and government regulatory powers as essential instruments for controlling the recurrent crises of capitalism. However, these programmes were toned down in practice, partly as a consequence of the failure of the expected depression to materialise, and partly because of a loss of votes to the bourgeois parties which represented the new Social Democratic line as a departure from the accommodating stance of the immediate prewar years. From the late 1940s until about the end of the 1960s, the fundamental strategy of Scandinavian Social Democratic administrations has been simultaneously

Table 1.4 Election results (percentage of total vote) and government composition in Denmark, Norway and Sweden, 1945-77

(a) *Denmark*

Year	Comm.	SF	SD	Rad.	Lib.	Cons.	CD	Prog.	Other	Govt. Party
1945	12.5		32.8	8.2	23.4	18.2			4.9	Lib.
1947	6.8		40.0	6.9	27.6	12.4			6.3	SD
1950	4.6		39.6	8.2	21.3	17.8			8.5	Lib.+Cons.
1953(a)	4.8		40.4	8.6	22.1	17.3			6.8	
1953(b)	4.3		41.3	7.8	23.1	16.8			6.7	SD
1957	3.1		39.4	7.8	25.1	16.6			8.0	SD+Rad.(M)
1960	1.1	6.1	42.1	5.8	21.1	17.9			5.9	SD+Rad.(M)
1964	1.2	5.8	41.9	5.3	20.8	20.1			5.7	SD
1966	0.8	10.9	38.3	7.3	19.3	18.7			4.7	SD
1968	1.0	6.1	34.2	15.0	18.6	20.4			4.7	Bourgeois(M)
1971	1.4	9.1	37.3	14.4	15.6	16.7			5.5	SD
1973	3.6	6.0	25.6	11.2	12.3	9.2	7.8	15.9	8.4	Lib.
1975	4.2	5.0	30.0	7.1	23.3	5.5	2.2	13.6	9.1	SD
1977	3.7	3.9	37.0	3.6	12.0	8.5	6.5	14.6	10.2	SD

Key: Comm. = Communist; SF = Socialist People's Party; SD = Social Democrats; Rad. = Radical-Liberals; Lib. = Liberal; Cons. = Conservatives; CD = Centre Democrats; Prog. = Progress Party; Bourgeois = coalition of Rad. + Lib. + Cons.; M = government with parliamentary majority

(b) *Norway*

Year	Comm.	SPP	Lab.	CPP	Lib.	Cons.	Cen.	ALP	Other	Govt. Party
1945	11.9		41.0	7.9	13.8	17.0	8.0		0.4	Lab.(M)
1949	5.8		45.7	8.4	12.4	15.9	4.9		6.9*	Lab.(M)
1953	5.1		46.7	10.5	10.0	18.4	8.8		0.5*	Lab.(M)
1957	3.4		48.3	10.2	9.6	16.8	8.6		3.1*	Lab.(M)
1961	2.9	2.4	46.8	9.3	7.2	19.3	6.8		5.4*	Lab.
									(4 weeks in 1963	Bourgeois)
1965	1.4	6.0	43.1	7.8	10.2	20.3	9.4		1.8*	Bourgeois(M)
1969	1.0	3.4	46.5	7.8	9.4	18.8	9.0		4.1*	Bourgeois(M)
	(Feb. 1971-Sept. 1972, minority Lab; Autumn 1972-3, CPP+Cen.)									
1973	11.2		35.3	12.2	3.5	17.4	11.0	5.0	4.4†	Lab.
1977	0.4	3.9	42.4	12.1	3.2	24.7	8.6		4.5	Lab.

Key: Comm. = Communist; SPP = Socialist People's Party; Lab. = Labour Party; CPP = Christian People's Party; Lib. = Liberal; Cons. = Conservative; Cen. = Agrarian/Centre Party; ALP = Anders Lange Party; Bourgeois = coalition of CPP+Lib.+ Cons.+Cen.; M = government with parliamentary majority
     *Consisting largely of Joint Non-Socialist lists.
     †Consisting largely of New People's Party, a splinter of the Liberal Party.

(c) *Sweden*

Year	Comm.	SAP	Cen.	Lib.	Mod.	Other	Govt. Party
1944	10.3	46.5	13.6	12.9	15.8	0.9	National
					(From July 1945		SAP*)
1948	6.3	46.1	12.4	22.7	12.3	0.2	SAP*
					(From Oct. 1951		SAP+Cen.(M))
1952	4.3	46.0	10.7	24.4	14.4	0.2	SAP+Cen.(M)
1956	5.0	44.6	9.5	23.8	17.1	0.0	SAP+Cen.(M)
					(From Oct. 1957		SAP*)
1958	3.4	46.2	12.7	18.2	19.5	0.0	SAP*
1960	4.5	47.8	13.6	17.5	16.6	0.0	SAP*
1964	5.2	47.3	13.2	17.0	13.7	3.6	SAP*
1968	3.0	50.1	15.7	14.3	12.9	4.0	SAP(M)
1970	4.8	45.3	19.9	16.2	11.5	2.3	SAP
1973	5.3	43.6	25.1	9.4	14.3	2.3	SAP
1976	4.8	42.7	24.1	11.1	15.6	1.7	Bourgeois(M)

Key: Comm. = Communist/Left-Party Communist; SAP = Social Democrats; Cen. = Agrarian Party/Centre Party; Lib. = Liberal; Mod. = Conservatives/Moderate Unity Party; Bourgeois = coalition of Cen.+Lib.+Mod; M = government with lower house majority

*Having a majority or parity of votes when taking into account joint votes of the two parliamentary chambers.

to foster the widest possible collaboration with non-socialist forces and to build on the unity and integration of the labour movement with the aim of facilitating the rapid expansion of the economic resources required to finance an expansive programme of social reform. The extent to which this strategy has been successful in the achievement of its ultimate objective is the subject of the next chapter, but some discussion of the political mechanisms by which it has been pursued is a necessary preliminary for an adequate assessment of the performance of the Scandinavian Social Democratic parties during their long tenure in office.

Inherent in the Social Democratic strategy has been the belief that the combination of increasing disposable incomes and constant, although gradual, social amelioration, both made possible by economic growth, provided a sure foundation for continued electoral success. In general, this expectation has been fulfilled. Table 1.4 shows the details of all the parliamentary elections taking place in Denmark, Norway and Sweden in the period 1944-77, and the composition of the resulting governments. Although it is apparent that there has been a real decline in Social Democratic electoral stability during the 1970s, the preceding quarter century was characterised by a relatively unchanging pattern of electoral support. In those twenty-five years, the Swedish Social Democrats were in office continuously, either alone or in coalition with

the Agrarians; the Norwegian Labour Party formed single-party governments for twenty years, and the Danish Social Democrats, although
always in a minority or reliant on coalition arrangements, were a party
of government for eighteen years.

This record of governmental success has been in part a consequence
of the ability of the Social Democratic parties to institutionalise mechanisms for collaboration between organised social groupings. As will be
noted a a later stage of the analysis, such mechanisms have venerable
antecedents in each of the Scandinavian countries but, since the 1930s
they have become an integral part of virtually every area of social and
political life. Whenever possible, decisions are taken in consultation
with the relevant organised interests. This so-called 'corporate pluralism'
can, as Stein Rokkan has pointed out, lead to a situation in which the
balance of group interests is as significant an aspect of democratic
decision-making as the electoral process itself.

> The crucial decisions on economic policy are rarely taken in the
> parties or in Parliament: the central area is the bargaining table
> where the government authorities meet directly with the trade union
> leaders, the representatives of the farmers, the smallholders, and the
> fishermen, and the delegates of the Employers' Association. These
> yearly rounds of negotiations have in fact come to mean more in the
> lives of rank-and-file citizens than the formal elections (Rokkan,
> 1966, p. 107).

Although this comment was made in the Norwegian context, Social
Democratic and, more recently, bourgeois, administrations in Denmark
and Norway have similarly attempted to involve a wide spectrum of
groups in the rule-making process.[14]

Despite the fact that the mechanisms of corporate pluralism can
have the effect of diminishing the role of parties and parliament, they
are also, in essence, the instrument of policy-making within the parliamentary arena. This is hardly surprising in so far as the major interest
divisions in Scandinavain society — trade unions, farmers, Free Church/
temperance and employers — are also reflected in the fragmentation of
the party system — Social Democrats, Centre (Liberals in Denmark),
Liberals (plus Christian People's Party in Norway; the Radical-Liberals
in Denmark have a rather more secular emphasis) and Conservatives
(see Rustow, 1956, p. 176). Moreover, legislation in Scandinavia is
generally initiated by the presentation of the report of a royal commis-
sion representing all interested sections of opinion, is then tendered for
comment to the relevant interest groups, and is decided on by the deli-
berations of a parliamentary committee, whose major aim is to produce
proposals which can be *unanimously* agreed by the plenary body.

These procedures have important consequences for the style of political life in the Scandinavian countries. First, they make collaboration an intrinsic aspect of virtually all policy making. Very occasionally, the majority party may try to force its proposals through against the strenuous opposition of substantial sectors of organised opinion but, more usually, proposals which cannot be formulated in a mutually acceptable manner are put in abeyance pending a more favourable political climate. Second, although change effected through such a corporate mechanism tends to be rather gradual, it is also almost irreversible. Because legislation is the result of genuine accommodations between organised groups, and within parliamentary committees, those who contribute to its formulation take a responsibility for its substance. The general rule of Scandinavian politics is that changes of government do not involve dramatic reversals of previous legislation. Finally, such a mechanism permits even persistent minority and coalition governments, of the kind which have existed continuously in Denmark during the postwar period, to govern with a high degree of effectiveness (Damgaard, 1974, p. 115). Although the governmental party or parties many not have a parliamentary majority, they see their major function as the production of legislation which achieves the optimum balance between their own party programmes and a parliamentary consensus. Naturally, the fact that Social Democracy has been somewhat weaker in Denmark than elsewhere in Scandinavia has been reflected in policy output, but its position as the major governing party within the context of the system of corporate pluralism has ensured that pressures for social reform have had a significant impact. The end result of politics by corporate pluralism has been to give a permanent voice to the industrial and political wings of the labour movement within the counsels of government. For much of the time it has been the predominant voice, and in virtue of the system of institutionalised collaboration, it is a voice which remains extremely influential even when in a minority or in opposition.

The voice of the labour movement is given additional force to the extent that is speaks with a single tongue. This is, of course, the major reason that the unity and integration of the labour movements in Scandinavia has figured so largely in the previous discussion. Within the context of the corporate pluralist system, the complementary nature of the aims and organisational effort of the two basic components of the labour movements in Scandinavia has been a crucial mechanism of continued Social Democratic ascendancy. Based on the confidence that the political arm of the labour movement will always give whole-hearted priority to full-employment policy and the pursuit of fresh reform initiatives, the trade unions have been willing to accept the need to avoid unnecessary industrial conflict and to co-operate in fulfilling the government's economic growth strategy. Thus, as Walter Galenson has put it: 'Contemporary Scandinavian socialism is essentially collective bargaining transplanted to the political arena; its strength lies in its ability to augment worker welfare with the minimum of social conflict' (Galenson, 1968, p. 155).

A complete catalogue of the forms that the postwar integration of the Scandinavian labour movements have taken would require a large book of its own, but a few examples will suffice to show the depth of the co-operation and its implications for the success of the governments economic and industrial policies.[15] After 1945 the trade unions colla- borated fully in postwar reconstruction. Since the Norwegian Labour government took a very firm line that the first priority must be a rate of industrial investment which continued at a high level not merely in the immediate reconstruction period, but for the forseeable future, this involved real sacrifices for the working people, which the trade unions felt were justified in terms of eventual benefits to their members.

> Organized labor in Norway has accepted the goal of a high-invest- ment, low-consumption economy with all that means for wage and other economic policies because organized labor approves the general economic objectives of the Norwegian Labor Party and the Norwegian Labor government. After the high-investment economy has been in operation for a number of years and the Norwegian economy has been converted from a relatively underdeveloped to a mature industrial economy, organized labor would then expect the government to shift back to the goal of a high-consumption, low-investment economy in which a high and expanding standard of living would be widely shared (Gruchy, 1966, p. 325).

The former part of this expectation has now been amply fulfilled with a high average level of private consumption *per capita*, and the trade unions show few signs of disappointment that Norway still has one of the highest rates of investment in Western Europe.

Economic growth is not merely a question of high investment levels, but is also crucially dependent on a high general level of industrial pro- ductivity. In Sweden, LO provided much of the intellectual impetus for the Social Democratic government's implementation of an 'active' labour market policy designed to foster the structural rationalisation of industry.[16] This policy has subsequently been adopted in Norway and, to a lesser extent, in Denmark. 'Active' labour market policy brings together a large number of labour-movement economic and social ob- jectives, some of which will be mentioned in the context of the next chapter. It starts from the assumption that a small country which lives by exporting can only become richer by enhancing its productivity.

This, in turn, means shifting resources from declining industries to those earning greater returns on capital. In the traditional, neo-classical view, this would happen automatically by capitalists seeking a higher rate of return on their investments; in reality, argued LO economists, the labour market stabilised at a point well below optimum productivity, since workers were willing to accept low wage rates, partly because of the fear of sinking into the reserve army of the unemployed and, more applicably in contemporary Scandinavian conditions, because of various non-economic attachments which were conducive to inertia. At this point, the desire to remove the structural impediments to higher industrial productivity ties in with the wage-levelling aims implicit in the LO's 'wage policy of solidarity'. By utilising the unions' centralised bargaining strength progressively to push up the wage rates of the lower paid relative to the general wage level, the least productive firms would be forced out of business. Such a policy implied that the trade union were willing to countenance some degree of structural unemployment so long as it was *temporary*. The transient character of such unemployment was to be guaranteed by the final feature of the 'active' labour market policy: the government's responsibility to use selective measures to stimulate full employment and to provide generous benefits for those temporarily out of work, as well as adequate facilities for industrial retraining. It seems fair comment to suggest that the progressive elaboration of this policy since the 1950s had made a major contribution to the high levels of productivity and low levels of unemployment which have characterised the Swedish and Norwegian economies in the last two decades.[17]

Denmark has also experimented with an 'active' labour market policy since the 1960s, although, as measured by the level of unemployment, with rather less success than either Sweden of Norway.[18] This relative failure owes at least something to a certain reluctance on the part of administrations of varying political complexions purposively to manipulate the market mechanism. Thus, a 1974 report by OECD examiners criticises 'a general belief amongst the authorities that Labour market problems in Denmark will, in the future as they have in the past, solve themselves with minimal State intervention' (OECD, 1974a, p. 36). However, the failure also reflects a fundamental weakness in the Danish economy and its organisational basis. From the 1950s onward, the situation has been characterised by a relatively low level of economic growth, periodic unemployment, a serious balance of payments deficit and tendency toward inflation. These problems, which are so reminiscent of the recent British experience, have their origins in rather similar structural conditions: the traditional division into small-scale units of production stemming from the early experience of industrialisation, and the consequent proliferation of semi-autonomous trade unions and employers' organisations (see Elvander, 1974, pp. 419-22).

The most recent stage in the utilisation of labour movement solidarity as a mechanism of Social Democratic economic strategy has been the attempt to create viable incomes policies to cope with the novel economic problems of the 1970s. Here, too, the structural weakness of the Danish trade unions in comparison with the rest of Scandinavia has made for considerable difficulties. Strangely enough, the Danish authorities' unwillingness to manipulate the labour market has never been paralleled by a similar disinclination to intervene actively in wage disputes. As previously noted, the most significant element of the political settlement of the early 1930s was the government's legislative action to prevent wage reductions, and it has long been standard practice to resolve wage disputes by means of state mediation. However, in a sense, the frequency of government intervention has involved an admission of weakness on the part of the labour market 'partners', since it has demonstrated their incapacity to reach agreements binding on their constituent organisations. Throughout the 1960s, Social Democratic governments had difficulties in persuading LO to go all the way with its economic stabilisation proposals. At the end of 1962 a joint initiative by the Social Democrats and LO nearly succeeded, but negotiations eventually broke down, and the government imposed a two-year legislative settlement to stabilise both wages and profits. Under circumstances of continuing inflation, it has been progressively harder for LO to persuade its loosely integrated membership that higher wage costs were seriously affecting Denmark's competitive position. In 1973 amicable relations within the labour movement reached a new low with a thirteen-day general strike directed against a minority Social Democratic administration. The need for continued wage restraint remains a serious weakness for the Danish labour movement, although, in fairness, it should be noted that policy collaboration between the Social Democrats and LO on such issues as the improvement of the work environment and economic democracy is so close that the standpoints of the two organisations are virtually indistinguishable.

Incomes policy in Norway and Sweden has been more successful than in Denmark, both as a consequence of more favourable economic circumstances and because the greater centralised authority of the labour market organisations has obviated the need for imposed legislative settlements. What has taken place since about 1974 has been the elaboration of established corporate agreements within a framework of government guarantees. As ever, in the Scandinavian context, the primary guarantee has been in regard to full employment. In a period of worldwide recession, counter-cyclical policy has been used to ensure that unemployment has not risen above a maximum of 2 per cent. It is easy to attribute Norway's ability to counter recessionary tendencies to her good fortune in being able to offset a balance-of-payments deficit against future oil revenues but, as Norway's Secretary-General to the Ministry of Finance argues, this cannot account for Sweden's successful use of a similar policy.

> Sweden has implemented a sizeable counter-cyclical policy and succeeded in maintaining a high level of employment. The Swedish policy has, however, been more cautious than the policy in Norway. If we had been in the same situation as Sweden, we would have pursued a policy similar to the one we are pursuing now, but we would — as the Swedes — have been somewhat more cautious. Probably we would not have increased the disposable real income as much as we have done, and we would have had to concentrate more on less import-intensive capital formation and consumption (Erichsen, 1976, p. 16).

Given the basic guarantee of full employment, the trade unions have collaborated in policies designed to reduce cost inflation, mainly through accepting real wage increases in the form of reduced direct taxation and increased transfer payments rather than higher personal income.

This has created greater problems for the trade unions than were at first foreseen. It has to some extent been difficult to convince the membership that gains which are not reflected in pre-tax incomes can be genuine. As Assar Lindbeck notes, a consequence of the Swedish incomes settlement of 1974, which led to a 7 per cent increase in average real incomes, was that 'considerable dissatisfaction was expressed by labour union members over an "unfavourable" outcome of bargaining!' (Lindbeck, 1975, p. 328). The trade union leadership has also progessively become more disenchanted with a form of wage negotiation which is exclusively political and undermines the trade unions' traditional collective bargaining functions. By the Spring of 1977, there are clear signs that incomes settlements of this type have a very limited future in Sweden and Norway, although, in the latter country at least, they are acknowledged to have had a significant impact on inflationary tendencies (OECD, 1977, p. 37).

Accommodation to a wide range of social forces through the institutionalisation of corporate pluralism and the ability to build on the integration and unity of the labour movement have by no means been the only mechanisms by which the Scandinavian Social Democratic parties have tried to maintain their political ascendancy in the postwar period. In one sense, this presentation has been seriously one-sided in so far as it has left for later discussion the substance of the social welfare reforms and egalitarian policies, which, far more than its role as an agency of social harmony and economic growth, would constitute the basis for each Social Democratic party's self-assessment of its distinctive achievement and its claim on the loyalty of the electorate. Nevertheless, the willingness to arrive at compromises with groupings representing non-working-class interests and the harnessing of labour movement solidarity to the cause of enhanced economic growth have been considered as essential preconditions of a continuing social reform policy within the context of a democratic society. Together, they would provide the votes and resources for a slow, but inevitable, socialist transformation. Certainly, until the mid-1960s, they seemed a sound basis for Social Democratic electoral victory. Since that time, this has appeared less certain, and it is to the political reasons for this development that the last section of this chapter is devoted.

1.5 New problems and new parties

Between the 1920s and the late 1960s there was an extraordinary stability in the Scandinavian party system. The basic situation was the confrontation of an increasingly dominant Social Democratic party and three bourgeois parties — Conservatives, Liberals (Radical-Liberals in Denmark) and Agrarians (Liberals in Denmark). In this period, the only appreciable party to gain a permanent foothold in the parliamentary arena was the Norwegian Christian People's Party. Since this party was an offshoot of the old Liberal alliance, which had democratised the political system in the latter part of the nineteenth century, it easily found a natural role as a part of the bourgeois line-up. After the early 1920s, leftist parties had tended to fade away in face of growing Social Democratic support, and it was only in 1944-5 that the Communists made any great inroads into the democratic socialist vote. This wartime enthusiasm for the Communist Party as part of the anti-Hitler alliance rapidly dwindled in the 'cold war' period and, in the late 1940s, Social Democratic trade-union leaders waged a bitter, although generally successful, campaign to extirpate Communist influence within the unions. Finally, in surveying the stability of the Scandinavian party systems, it is appropriate to note that Denmark's low electoral threshold permitted a number of very small parties to gain temporary representation, and, indeed, that the Justice Party entered into the majority Social Democratic and Radical-Liberal coalitions of the late 1950s and early 1960s. Despite the existence of such minor parties, the Danish situation into the latter part of the 1960s could be summarised by the conclusion that 'the parties of the 1920s have by and large kept their dominant position in the electorate, in Parliament and, we might add, at the cabinet level par excellence' (Damgaard, 1974, p. 107).

The stability of the Scandinavian party systems began to show signs of lessening in the 1960s. The old ideological issues which had divided the Social Democrats and bourgeois parties came to have a lesser salience as policy was progressively determined by mutual accommodations through the corporate pluralist system. The policy outputs resulting from the use of this decision-making mechanism, and the very nature of the mechanism itself, created new problems for a variety of social groups. To some degree these problems have led to the emergence of new parties and new party alignments. Moreover, even where the established party system has retained a monumental stability, as in Sweden, new issues have concerned the electorate, and this has affected the strengths of the respective parties. New parties, party alignments and political issues present a challenge to the established Social Democratic strategy outlined in the previous section. To remain in power and to pursue their social reform aims requires a radical rethinking of the policy options open to a democratic socialist party in the latter decades of the twentieth century. Something of the emerging Social Democratic response in social policy terms will be discussed in the next chapter, but a summary of the new problems and parties that occupy the contemporary political arena provides the necessary perspective for that discussion.

The first portent of the emergence of issues and parties which might disturb the Social Democrats' dominant position in the Scandinavian party system was the election of eleven Socialist People's Party representatives in Denmark in 1960, and two in Norway in 1961. The basis for the appearance of a significant presence to the left of the Social Democrats had been laid in the immediate postwar years by those countries' abandonment of a neutral stance in foreign relations. After abortive negotiations between all the Scandinavian nations concerning the possibility of a Nordic Defence Pact, Denmark and Norway joined NATO in 1949, while Sweden reaffirmed her longstanding neutrality policy. Amongst a substantial minority of the Norwegian Labour Party, the abandonment of the Nordic option revived strong radical feelings of a kind which had been quiescent since the 1920s. In Denmark, Social Democratic voices were somewhat less strident in attacking the leadership's pro-NATO line, and it was the strongly neutralist Radical-Liberal Party which formed the major focus of opposition. In each case, the new defence policy was guaranteed acceptance by the support of the major bourgeois parties.[19] The resentments aroused by the departure in foreign policy had no realistic outlet while Stalinist Communist parties provided the only socialist alternative to Social Democratic allegiance. However, in the late 1950s, Aksel Larsen, a leading figure within the Danish Communist Party, took Khrushchev's remarks on separate 'party roads to socialism' rather more seriously than may have been intended by their author, and advocated a revisionist line combining Danish democratic practices, militant socialism and neutralism. When he was expelled by the Communist Party, he founded the Socialist People's Party. Almost immediately thereafter, a similar initiative was taken by Norwegian radical Leftists.

Although the Danish Socialist People's Party was the larger of the two, it was the Norwegian Party which first dented the façade of Social Democratic ascendancy. The 1961 Norwegian parliament was divided equally between the Labour Party and the bourgeois parties with the two Socialist People's Party members holding the balance. In theory, the new left-wing party was helpless, since to install a bourgeois government for any appreciable period was the last thing it wanted. However, in 1963, the Socialist People's Party served notice that its allegiance could not be taken for granted by voting against the government. As a consequence, for one month Norway had its first non-socialist government since the Liberation. In Norway, as events were to prove, the Socialist People's support was based almost entirely on foreign policy issues, and the Party failed to increase its representation in 1965 and disappeared as a parliamentary party in 1969. In the years 1970-3, it made an astonishing recovery as a result of the major divisions within the Labour Party over entry into the European Economic Community. Those on the Left, whether they were unreformed Communists, adherents of the Social People's Party or members of the Labour Party, saw the EEC as a 'capitalist demon', which would prevent Norway's progress, however gradual, towards a truly socialist society (Heidar, 1977, pp. 297-8). In the 1972 referendum, the Labour leadership and parts of a very divided trade union movement, together with the Conservative Party and the Employers' Federation were soundly defeated by an alliance composed of the radical Left, a section of the Liberal Party, and the Christian and Centre parties. In the 1973 election, Labour suffered their worst electoral defeat since 1930, and formed a minority administration dependent on the support of a Socialist Electoral Alliance, which brought together all those elements of the radical Left that had campaigned so successfully against entry into the Common Market.

The Danish Socialist People's Party took longer to have their first significant impact on the political scene. However, the severe economic difficulties experienced by Denmark, and the greater opportunities for exerting left-wing influence in the trade unions as a consequence of their low degree of centralisation by Scandinavian standards, provided fertile soil for attracting electoral support on domestic as well as foreign policy issues. In 1966, for the first time in Danish political history, the combined Left — the Social Democrats and Socialist People's Party —

won a parliamentary majority. Although differences between these parties on EFTA, relationships with the European Community and the general pace of reform, did not permit the formation of a majority coalition, there was a decided leftward shift in the policy stance of the new Social Democratic minority administration, and the contact committee set up for liaison between the parties of the Left became popularly known as the 'red cabinet'.[20] The most important consequence of this limited collaboration was to disrupt the basis of the party alignment which had prevailed for more than fifty years. For the first time the Radical-Liberals found that they had greater common interests with the Liberals and the Conservatives than with the Social Democrats. In 1968, the bourgeois parties won a major electoral victory, and formed a majority coalition which was to last for more than three years.

When, in late 1971, the Left again won a slight parliamentary majority, it seemed that the scene was set for a new alignment in which the Left, composed predominantly of the Social Democrats but spurred to a new radicalism by the Socialist People's Party, would compete with a united bourgeois front. There were, however, important differences between the parties of the Left. In particular, the Social Democrats, precisely because the more radical Leftists were outside the Party, were relatively united in their desire to join the European Economic Community, which, with the accession of Britain, would include Denmark's major trading partners outside Scandinavia. Thus, until the latter part of 1972, when a referendum gave a decisive 'yes' to entry, the Social Democratic minority government relied heavily on the bourgeois parties to sustain it in parliament. Thereafter, the Social Democratic Party, with a new, and somewhat left-inclined leader, Anker Jørgensen, attempted to tread a cautious path between the political extremes. However, this political balancing act failed and, in 1973, a moderate faction seceded from the Social Democrats to form the Centre Democratic Party. In the election of that year, the Social Democrats, stripped down to hard-core support, polled a mere 25 per cent. Since then the Left, fragmented into several small competing parties and unable to influence a Social Democratic Party, has been forced into a left-centre stabilising role in a party system now almost completely fractionalised.

In Sweden, in contrast, the Left has had a much less impact on the political system. In the 1960s, the Communist Party changed its name to the Left-Party Communist in order to symbolise its adherence to the democratic road to socialism. The upsurge of New Left enthusiasm during the latter part of the decade seemed to offer fair prospects for the 1968 election, but the Soviet invasion of Czechoslovakia made potential Social Democratic deserters return to the fold. During the first half of the 1970s, a parliamentary situation in which the Social

Democrats were heavily dependent on Left-Party Communist support to ensure survival may well have influenced the noticeably more radical Social Democratic policy stance in this period. However, the Left-party Communist's showing in the 1976 election was extremely disappointing, and, following a split in early 1977, it seems quite possible that neither fragment of the Party will be able to surmount the 4 per cent electoral threshold required for parliamentary representation.

The reasons for the widely divergent impact of leftist parties in Scandinavia since the early 1960s are inherent in the history and structure of the respective labour movements. The fundamental premis on which the allegiance of the Social Democratic Left-wing has been based has been the independent national status of the Scandinavian countries, which permitted a gradual transition to socialism depending only on the willingness of the electorate to embrace progressive ideas. Both NATO and EEC have been seen as wholly capitalist institutions, whose embrace would irrevocably bind the Scandinavian countries to an exploitative economic system. Thus, the crucial difference between the Scandinavian nations has been Sweden's unwillingness to contemplate any basic departure from her traditional policy of military and economic non-alignment. Norway's leftist explosion in 1970-3 was clearly, directly related to the EEC issue, and now that has been shelved for the foreseeable future, the opinion polls have shown a strong trend away from the Socialist Electoral Alliance and back to the Labour Party.[21] Unless the Left can find some dramatic new issue before the election of September 1977, their previous victory is likely to be relegated to a minor historical footnote. What differentiates the Danish from the Norwegian experience is that issues relating to Denmark's freedom of action in the international sphere have been joined to economic weaknesses and a labour movement lacking the tradition of solidarity to be found in the other Scandinavian countries. Once the EEC question was resolved, the Norwegian LO was quickly able to restore unity and its traditional links with the Labour Party. In Denmark, however, trade unionists supporting the Communist and Socialist People's parties have played an active role in opposing many of the economic policies of the present minority Social Democratic administration. Given the relatively lower level of labour movement solidarity in Denmark, and the intense fragmentation of the party system, which, as will be shown, has causes other than the Socialist People's Party's attack on the left flank of the Social Democrats, a number of small parties of the Left are likely to be a significant feature of Danish politics for some time to come.

Another new issue which has emerged to threaten continued Social Democratic ascendancy within the Scandinavian political systems has been the problems involved in financing the welfare state. Without trespassing unduly on the subject of the next chapter, it is clear that since 1960 there has not only been an increase in the level of social security expenditure in monetary terms, but also a virtual doubling of of the percentage of National Income devoted to that purpose. This, combined with a vast increase in educational, health and social welfare spending, has led to a commensurate growth in the burden imposed by taxation and social security contributions. Since direct taxation is progressive, and given the impact of inflation in pushing ever lower strata of the incomes pyramid into the higher tax brackets, this development has had the effect of making the taxation issue salient not merely to the higher income groups in society, but also to wide middle sections, including industrial workers, whose marginal tax rates are now well in excess of 50 per cent.

Here is an issue apparently tailor-made for exploitation by the bourgeois parties. A high level of taxation, and its distinctive effects on thrift and initiative, have always been the themes most stressed by middle-class parties opposed to extensive programmes of public spending. The paradox of the Scandinavian situation, and the reason that the taxation issue has become a problem for the stability of the party systems, as well as for the continued dominance of the Social Democrats, is that the distaste felt by the bourgeois parties and their supporters for high marginal rates of taxation has not been matched by a comparable distaste for public spending. A number of factors contribute to the explanation of this paradox. In Scandinavia as elsewhere, social welfare spending has to some extent become a process of competitive counterbidding for the allegiance of the marginal voter. To the degree that politics has become an auction, there is an inherent tendency to the expansion of public spending. The corporate pluralist mechanism has also contributed to this process in so far as compromises are most easily reached when each party to the bargain gains at least something. The operational rule of the Caucus-race is that 'Everybody has won, and all must have prizes' (Carroll, 1865). Moreover, it would be wholly unfair to the bourgeois parties not to point out that, in the course of four decades of Social Democratic dominance, they have become almost completely won over to the ideal of the humane welfare society.[22] That conversion is the more genuine in that the Centre and Liberal parties have a significant constituency in social groups that are not appreciably better rewarded than the average industrial worker.

A commitment to the welfare state has not prevented the bourgeois parties from criticising the tax burden imposed by Social Democratic reform programmes and using electoral platforms to promise taxation changes to the advantage of the middle-income earner. The electoral victories of bourgeois parties in Norway in 1965, Denmark in 1968 and

Sweden in 1976 must, at least in part, be interpreted as a measure of the appeal of such promises. The problem for the resulting bourgeois coalition administrations has been in keeping their promises. In both Norway and Denmark, growth of public expenditure actually accelerated during the bourgeois parties' tenure of office and with it the burden of taxation. With the relative failure of the bourgeois parties to provide an outlet for the voter disturbed by the high personal costs of social reform programmes, the political ground was prepared for the emergence of new parties opposing the whole system which resulted in the monolithic social welfare consensus of the established parties.

In the Autumn of 1972, a Danish lawyer by the name of Glistrup founded the Progress Party, whose programme marked a dramatic departure in the style and content of Danish politics.

> The Progress Party aimed at abolishing income tax by drastic cuts in public expenditure. Opposition to state interference in the economy was underpinned by violent verbal attacks on public servants, who were accused of being underproductive and overpaid papershufflers. Other established institutions got their share of criticism too: The old parties were referred to as being senile (Nielsen, 1976, p.147).

Against many predictions, the Party has seemingly established a permanent and major role in politics — it is currently the largest party in the system apart from the Social Democrats — and has obtained more than 13 per cent of the vote in the last three general elections. In Norway, a similar, though rather less vitriolic, party contested the 1973 election. The Anders Lange Party, named after its founder, obtained 5 per cent of the vote and four parliamentary mandates. With the death of Anders Lange in 1974, it is extremely unlikely that a specifically anti-tax party will make any impact in the 1977 election. In Sweden, the uninterrupted rule of the Social Democrats has, until the present, left the bourgeois parties as the unchallenged protagonist of a more moderate tax burden. Whether that will still be the case at the conclusion of the bourgeois parties' first term in office remains to be seen.

A full explanation of the success of the Progress Party lies outside the scope of this study, but some remarks are in order in so far as the phenomenon has causes and consequences which have implications for the role of Social Democracy in the party system.[23] As will be shown in the next chapter, the level of welfare expenditure in the three Scandinavian countries is rather similar. The differences between the countries lie in the differential capacity to finance such expenditure. The Danish situation has been exacerbated by the need to run up a large balance-of-payments deficit to finance expanding private and public consumption, and the already mentioned failure to pursue a viable incomes policy. The technique of increasing real wages by means of cuts in direct taxation, adopted by both Norwegian and Swedish Social Democratic administrations in recent years, has not only had the objective of preventing excessive increases in wage costs, but also of keeping taxation within reasonable bounds. Danish governments have been much less able to increase real incomes, and partly because of this, and partly because of the insufficient solidarity of the labour movement, have also been unable to gain collaboration in shifting the tax burden somewhat from direct to indirect taxation.[24] One consequence of this has been that large numbers of industrial workers now fall within tax brackets in which welfare state 'costs in the form of high levels of taxation begin to exceed benefits from state transfers and collective consumption' (Hibbs, 1976, p. 45). Under these circumstances it is, perhaps, hardly surprising that the Progress Party has recruited support from former Social Democratic voters as well as cutting into the bourgeois electorate (Borre, 1974, p. 203).

The first effect of the dramatic growth of the Progress Party, together with the defection of the Centre Democrats, was the Social Democratic electoral debacle in 1973. However, the unwillingness of all the established parties to have any dealings with an anti-system party, has left the Social Democrats in a pivotal role as a major stabilising factor in the fragmented party system. This has been demonstrated by the Party's increased share of the electorate in both the 1975 and 1977 elections, which can most readily be interpreted as a desire for 'a return to normalcy'. It is also shown in a margin of Social Democratic relative dominance higher than at any time since the Second World War. In Denmark's precarious economic and parliamentary position, the other established parties have little option but to collaborate with the Social Democrats in holding the system together. However, in the long-term, Social Democratic prospects must depend on the creation of a new strategy for advancing democratic socialist aims within the constraints imposed by Denmark's precarious economic position and the structural weaknesses of the Danish labour movement.[25]

There is one final set of issues which have had a significant impact in the Scandinavian countries in recent years: those concerning the centralisation of power, resources, and population. These issues stem directly from the mechanisms utilised by the Social Democrats to ensure their political ascendancy over many decades. Corporate pluralism and the rationalisation of industrial production have increasingly been seen by critics as twin instruments of the dehumanisation of society and its decision-making processes. Such mechanisms may procure temporary social harmony and industrial efficiency, but they do so only at the

cost of depriving individuals of the capacity to determine their own life
chances, allowing industry to despoil the environment, and subordinat-
ing human frailties to the imperatives of the technocratic society. For
those who hold views of this kind, the solutions lie in decentralising
decision-making, preventing the further depopulation of rural areas, and
making industry pay greater attention to ecological considerations and
the social costs it imposes on the individual by rationalised work
processes.

In terms of future alignments in Scandinavian politics, the fascinating
aspect of the decentralisation issue is that it brings together such a diverse
range of political opinions. The parties which embrace the decentralisation idea most wholeheartedly are those of the extreme Left and the
Centre. In Sweden, it is the Left-Communist Party and the Centre Party
which are wholly opposed to the use of nuclear energy for power generation, because neither are willing to concede that the industrial advantages outweigh the potentially catastrophic social costs. In Norway, it
is the Socialist Electoral Alliance, the Centre Party and the Christian
People's Party which are reluctant 'to go for growth' on the strength of
oil revenues because of their fears that inadequate safety-precautions
might lead to environmental pollution on a massive scale. Naturally, the
emphasis of Left and Centre vary. The former are more concerned about
a capitalist conspiracy against a population made helpless by the collaboration of organised labour and industrial capital, whilst the latter
emphasise the system's failure to consider the real costs to individuals
of a rationalised and centralised industrial society. Despite such differences, the critics have in common an opposition to the untrammeled
imperatives of the industrial system of which the Social Democrats *and*
Conservatives may be seen as the chief proponents. Any speculation
about future party alignments which could bring the Left and Centre
into closer alliance might seem absurd until one remembers the Norwegian referendum on entry into the European Community in which it
was precisely the alliance of these forces which defeated the Conservatives and Social Democrats, who, in the eyes of their opponents, were
ready to sell out Norway to industrial (the emphasis of the Centre)
capitalism (the emphasis of the Left).

The Norwegian Labour Party has, as a consequence, become steadily
more sensitive to issues which might have a potential to unite Left and
Centre. The government has continually emphasised that North Sea oil
development must not expand at a pace which would disrupt the existing rural or industrial infrastructure. In Spring 1977, a blowout on the
Bravo Rig made the Labour Party rapidly reassess its timetable for permitting oil exploitation North of the sixty-second parallel. With an election only a few months away, the last impression it wished to give was

of a reckless disregard of the environment.

A similar sensitivity is likely to be shown by the Swedish Social Democratic Party in the future as a result of its defeat in the 1976 election. The most important manifestation of the decentralisation issue in Sweden has not been the unity of political opposites, but the steady growth of the Centre Party, which constitutes the most important change in the country's political firmament during the last decade. The Centre Party's success has been attributable to its abandonment of its former narrow role as a farmers' interest party, and its new self-conception as the party of decentralisation.

> [All] technology and activity in social and industrial life should
> be subordinated to the demand for an environment that is adapted
> to man's needs and capacities.
> The Centre Party considers that this aim can be realized only in
> a decentralized society (Party Programme, 1970, p. 3).

Between 1964 and 1973, the Party nearly doubled its share of the vote, and became the predominant influence in the bourgeois camp. In the 1976 election, a natural desire for change after forty-four years of one-party government, bourgeois promises of lower taxation for the middle-income earner, and bourgeois suggestions that the latest LO proposal for wage earners' funds amounted to wholesale socialisation of industry, all contributed to the defeat of the Social Democratic Party. However, almost certainly, the most significant single cause of the Social Democrats' final fall from grace was the Centre Party's single-minded campaign against the government's nuclear power policy, which was represented as an appalling danger to man and environment alike. The nuclear power option was seen as the natural culmination of the pursuit of a technocratic imperative imposed on an unwilling society by the 'faceless bureaucrats' of the corporate pluralist system. Thus, although Sweden's Social Democratic Party remained immune to the emergence of new parties and party alignments, Social Democratic political ascendancy could not remain forever untouched by new policy issues, the salience of which owed not a little to the repercussions of the mechanisms by which that ascendancy had been achieved.

2

Equality and welfare in capitalist society

In chapter 1, the emphasis was on the political achievements of the Scandinavian Social Democratic parties. It was suggested that the measure of these parties' political success compared with other Western European democratic socialist parties lay in two factors: their consistent ability to procure the support of approximately 40 per cent of the electorate and their high margin of relative dominance over political opponents. Together, these factors offered a *formal* explanation of the Scandinavian Social Democratic parties' exceptional record of office-holding, and gave reason to believe that, if anywhere, it would be in Scandinavia that the social reform programmes of democratic socialism would have the greatest *potential* for realisation.

Subsequent discussion of the stages of development through which the Scandinavian labour movements have acquired and maintained their political ascendancy stressed a number of features in common. In particular, there was an emphasis on the relative unity and integration of the Scandinavian labour movements, the evolution of an ideology focusing on social reform rather than social ownership, and the adoption of a strategy premised on class collaboration and the use of labour movement solidarity as mechanisms providing the resource base for reform. Differences in the development of the Scandinavian labour movements were also mentioned. These included the impact of variations in the timing and social context of development and dissimilarities in the nature of the democratisation process, which together have conditioned the extent of Social Democratic electoral support, party radicalism and labour movement solidarity. In general, the contrast between the Scandinavian countries showed the greater difficulties which the Danish Social Democratic Party has faced in reaping the political dividends of its chosen strategy and in countering the problems presented by new parties and party alignments in recent years.

Despite these differences, there is overwhelming evidence to justify the assertion that, until very recently, Scandinavian Social Democracy has been both politically successful *and* consistently reformist in orientation. However, such an assertion warrants no automatic inference that Social Democratic ascendancy is the *consequence* of reformist ideology and strategy. It is possible that Social Democracy in Scandinavia has been politically successful for reasons quite apart from its ideological stance. This is a topic which will be taken up in chapter 3. It is also possible that reformism is an ideology which has offered political dividends only in a specific historical period. This will be discussed at the conclusion of this chapter. Finally, it is possible that neither Social Democratic political ascendancy in Scandinavia nor a reformist strategy have produced results beneficial to the working class. This is the subject to which I will now turn.

2.1 Taking an agnostic approach

The claim of the Scandinavian Social Democratic parties has always been that, in adopting reformist means, they were in no sense adopting reformist goals. The objectives of a democratic socialist party remained those of any socialist party: a redistributive policy whose ultimate aim was a classless egalitarianism in which the principle of allocation would be 'from each according to his abilities, to each according to his needs'. Social Democratic ideologues do not generally argue that anything like such egalitarian society has been created in the Scandinavian countries, but rather that there has been gradual progress towards that end:

> we're far ahead compared to other countries. And we're far ahead compared to what Sweden looked like 30 or 40 years ago.
> But we have *not* gone very far if you want your dream of a classless society to come true. In that case, most of the work remains to be done! (Palme, in Vilgot Sjöman, 1968, p.33).

To the Party faithful that progress is manifested in many ways. Social Democratic welfare reforms — in the field of health provision, unemployment insurance, pensions, family maintenance, etc. — have contributed to the alleviation of the human misery that was once accepted as the inevitable concomitant of life in a capitalist society. Full employment policies combined with progressive taxation and the wage-levelling efforts of the trade unions have ensured that all wage earners have a real share in economic prosperity. Education is no longer the prerogative of a privileged minority, but is available to all who can and will benefit from it. Certainly, much remains to be done, but at least the gradual achievement of the past has been procured without violence and without the abandonment of democratic freedoms. Moreover, what remains to be done is only a question of time and the willingness to vote into power Social Democratic administrations dedicated to further egalitarian reform.

The Social Democratic claim that fundamental egalitarian reform — however gradual — is possible within the context of a democratic capitalist society has important implications. It contradicts the Marxist contention that democratic socialism will only be tolerated by the ruling class to the extent that it does not attempt to alter the basic reward structure of capitalism. Less obviously, it conflicts with the functionalist view in sociology that the stratification system in all modern industrial societies is determined by social parameters unamenable to political manipulation. Thus, as was noted in the preface, the extent of Scandinavian Social Democracy's achievement is inherently controversial since it touches on vital issues separating Right and Left wings of the European democratic socialist parties. It is no less so because it raises issues which divide contemporary social scientists. The problems inherent in the Social Democratic egalitarian claim are frequently discussed in highly polemical terms, but, as Frank Parkin so rightly points out, they demand 'a fairly agnostic approach . . . if we are to reach any satisfactory conclusions' (Parkin, 1971, p. 105).

Parkin himself provides such an approach in a chapter entitled *Social Democracy in Capitalist Societies*. Given the explicitly comparative status of the Social Democratic claim — i.e., 'we're far ahead of other countries' — he subjects it to comparative analysis. He examines data relating to the extent of social mobility, income distribution and welfare expenditure in a number of West European countries in order to assess whether democratic socialist ideology has had any consequences in egalitarian practice. Parkin's conclusions are almost wholly negative; Social Democracy does not live up to its claims. I shall devote some space to this argument not only because it has been extremely influential in informing British comment on the Scandinavian societies in recent years, but also because it shows some of the major criticisms to be answered in establishing a case for Scandinavian welfare achievement.

Parkin first examines the nature of social mobility opportunities and notes findings which suggest 'some connection between political ideology and social stratification' (Parkin, 1971, p. 109). The important mechanism here is, clearly, the educational system, and, whilst Parkin argues that the relatively high percentage of university students of working-class origin in Britain cannot be attributed to socialist administration since it occurred also in the prewar period, he notices that postwar educational reforms in Sweden and Norway make it 'reasonable to speak of a gradual improvement in the opportunity structure of the subordinate class brought about by direct political agency' (Parkin, 1971, p. 111). However, having admitted this, Parkin proceeds to argue that the expansion of mobility opportunities involves a *meritocratic* rather than an *egalitarian* conception of socialism. To offer working-class children the opportunity for enhanced mobility does not alter the reward structure of capitalism, but rather breaks the automatic linkage between particular families and particular positions in that structure. Moreover, the meritocratic interpretation may be even more conducive to efficient capitalist production because it implies a more efficient distribution of talent (Parkin, 1971, pp. 121-4).

That it is a meritocratic rather than an egalitarian structure which results from a Social Democratic ideology in action seems to be confirmed by Parkin's discussion of the reward structure itself. He presents data from a United Nations *Economic Survey of Europe in 1965* to show that there are considerable variations in the incomes distributions of advanced industrial societies, but that 'variations in the degree of equalization do not appear to be related to variations in government ideology' (Parkin, 1971, pp. 117-19). Parkin notes that direct taxation tends to be steeply progressive in many of these nations, but that it is less so in Norway and Sweden than in Britain. In addition, he cites evidence from the latter country that the overall impact of taxation is in fact, regressive, and that any tendencies towards income equalisation exhibited in the first postwar decade appear to have been *reversed*. By implication, he suggests that the situation in Scandinavia is likely to be rather similar. The contention that Social Democratic administrations have not succeeded in equalising the distribution of incomes is Parkin's most important criticism of the Social Democratic self-assessment of socialist achievement. It is the more crucial to the degree that he is correct in his assertion that '[the] distribution of occupational income gives us perhaps the best overall view of the reward structure, because for the great majority of the population the main or only source of income is from employment' (Parkin, 1971, p. 119). The validity of this contention is a topic to which I shall later return.

Finally, Parkin turns to the question of the impact of welfare and social security reforms. The data he presents again demonstrate that there are no dramatic differences between countries which have had democratic socialist administrations for long periods in the postwar era and those which have had governments predominantly of the Centre and Right. Parkin offers several explanations of this phenomenon. The adoption of welfare measures may be seen by the privileged as a form of capitalist social insurance against revolution and radicalism. It is arguable that 'the relatively low costs incurred by the dominant class in the provision of welfare are more than offset by the prevention of a more drastic kind of redistribution' (Parkin, 1971, pp. 124-5). Social security and welfare can also contribute to the efficiency of the capitalist mechanism; well-fed and healthy workers are more productive and docile than the 'huddled masses of the poor' who fuelled the furnaces of a nascent capitalism. Moreover, the social transfer payments which finance the welfare state may involve no net outlay to the privileged class.

> It seems to be the case that much of the distribution which does take place is of a 'horizontal' rather than a 'vertical' kind. That is, it is contributions from groups like the young or unmarried which are largely subsidizing payments to the sick or the elderly or those with large families. It is in other words, a form of 'life cycle' transfer, which does not necessarily entail much movement of resources from one *social class* to another (Parkin,1971, p. 125).

The welfare achievement of which the Scandinavian Social Democrats are so proud may amount to a Pyrrhic victory insofar as it contributes to the working class actually financing the greater security and efficiency of the capitalist system.

Parkin's argument leads to the conclusion that Social Democratic parties have become effectively deradicalised in the context of the modern democratic capitalist state. His agnostic approach appears to show Scandinavian Social Democratic egalitarian claims to be mere rhetoric; the Scandinavian countries have a reward structure which is in most respects similar to that imposed by the 'logic' of private ownership in other advanced industrial nations. To the degree that there are some minor dissimilarities which may be attributable to Social Democratic political intervention — in respect of greater educational opportunity and social welfare coverage — they are not only compatible with, but also conducive to, the enhanced efficiency of the capitalist system.

In what follows, I shall present data which in some respects conflict with Parkin's interpretation of the Scandinavian experience, but it is important to note that the status of the arguments presented is rather different. Parkin's interest is in whether Social Democratic ideology can lead to a fundamental transformation of the reward structure of capitalism, mine is in whether Social Democracy in Scandinavia has made a fundamental improvement in the condition of the working class. The data on which conclusions relating to either argument must be based are essentially similar, but the conclusions themselves need not be.

Educational mobility may be meritocratic, but it none the less permits working-class children to rise in the social hierarchy to a far greater extent than was possible for their parents.[1] Social welfare may redound to the advantage of the ruling class, but it is also manifestly to the advantage of the working class, to whom sickness, unemployment and old age are no longer the scourge they once were. It is because Parkin's argument in respect of social mobility and welfare does not *necessarily* imply that working-class conditions have not improved, that it was suggested that his most significant criticism of the Social Democratic achievement lies in the failure to procure a more egalitarian distribution of incomes.

The interest in Scandinavia seems to be contagious, and literary imagination somewhat lacking, judging by the recent publication of a comparative study of Britain and Sweden by Richard Scase, a colleague of Parkin's, with the title *Social Democracy in Capitalist Society*. The conclusions offered are rather similar except that Scase is rather less willing to make any concessions on the social mobility front.

[The] conclusion to be taken from investigations of social mobility in the two countries is that they are characterised by relatively common profiles; certainly, the position of manual workers is in no way fundamentally more advantageous in one society than in the other (Scase, 1977, p. 68).

Scase does emphasise Social Democratic educational reforms in Sweden, but he sees their failure to come to fruition in a changed stratification system as a further instance of what he considers to be the most serious contradiction of the Social Democratic era: the vast gap between the theoretical influence of a labour movement entrenched in power for many decades and its impotence to effect a major redistribution of social and economic rewards. According to Scase's survey findings of groups of British and Swedish workers, the latter, despite a higher absolute standard of living, show a greater degree of 'relative deprivation', which is manifested in 'heightened feelings of resentment' (Scase, 1977, p. 165). Such resentments are seen as a natural consequence of the dissonance between the labour movement's explicitly stated egalitarian goals and the failure in implementation. Scase suggests that recent signs of a renewed radicalism in Social Democratic Policy in Sweden may be seen as the leadership's response to rank-and-file resentments which might otherwise lead to a serious decline in working-class support.

The argument presented by Scase raises a fascinating problem of the sociology of electoral support: why should the working class continue to vote year after year for a party which fails to honour its promises? It seems strange to say the least but may, possibly, be explained by the fact that, although Scase devotes much attention to social and economic inequality in Britain and Sweden, he fails to compare rates of economic growth and the development of the welfare state. Fortunately, this latter omission is remedied elsewhere.

> In these ways, then, the Swedish labour movement has presented itself as the most important instrument of change and reform in society. Indeed, the achievements *have* been remarkable in terms of the provision of housing, pensions, welfare provisions, health, education and personal standards of living. It is arguable whether these accomplishments would have been attained without a long succession of Social Democratic governments, the development of accommodation between labour and capital, and the continued existence of the labour movement *as a movement* (Scase, 1976, p. 615).

Clearly, here, Scase provides excellent reasons for the continuing working-class support of the Swedish Social Democratic Party, although, at the same time, it is in a way which makes the 'heightened feelings of resentment' of Swedish workers more, rather than less, mysterious. It is, of course, possible that the reported findings regarding workers' attitudes are merely a rather unfortunate by-product of the small and unrepresentative samples interviewed by Scase.[2] However, it may also be possible that the Swedish workers' greater awareness of, and distaste for, economic and social inequalities may be less a symptom of 'relative deprivation', and more a manifestation of the class consciousness which has sustained the Swedish labour movement for more than half a century.

Both the studies so far examined focus primarily on the capacity of democratic socialist parties to alter the basic reward structures of capitalism, and both argue that similarities in the distribution of incomes, earnings and wealth, between countries with different records of democratic socialist political success, indicate how far short of their egalitarian claims such parties have fallen. This emphasis on reward structures is interesting since it provides a criterion for democratic socialist achievement which seems inherently more difficult to satisfy than many others which might have been chosen. The fundamental determinant of the reward structure of capitalism is the market mechanism, and it has been the premise of democratic socialist parties that it was possible to change the balance of social allocation in favour of the working class *without* the immediate and wholesale destruction of that mechanism. The acceptance of such a premise implies that egalitarian reform will be the more difficult to achieve the more directly the area of inequality concerned is a concomitant of market forces. However, the democratic socialist strategy has been to attempt to utilise the political power of the working-class movement increasingly to restrict the impact of the market in certain spheres, and so make them amenable to egalitarian redistritution. In particular, there has been an effort to make certain goods objects of collective or public rather than private consumption — health, education, community services, etc — and to reallocate benefits from wage earners to non-wage earners through child, unemployment and sickness benefits as well as old-age pensions. Such efforts to limit the impact of the market mechanism come under the common rubric of welfare state reforms. In a sense, an assessment of the capacity of the democratic socialist parties to effect welfare state reforms is a more important criterion of their achievement than is their impact on the reward structure of capitalism, since failure in the former respect would imply that democratic socialism was bereft of its rationale as a working-class party.

Comparisons of welfare state reforms require as agnostic an approach as do discussions of egalitarian incomes distribution. As the reader may have noticed, authors who agree in respect of one of these topics do not necessarily agree in respect of the other. Whilst Parkin suggests that data on welfare spending demonstrate no obvious connection between welfare spending and democratic socialist ideology, Scase argues strongly that many Swedish welfare achievements are directly attributable 'to a long succession of Social Democratic governments'. In general, the literature on welfare policy indicates that there are appreciable differences between nations in respect of welfare reform, but is not by any means agreed that these differences are a consequence of democratic socialist ideology.

In a pathfinding study of seventy-six nations, Phillips Cutright demonstrated that the most powerful explanation of differences in social security coverage was the level of social and economic development (Cutright, 1965). Subsequent studies have tended to confirm this finding, but, to the extent that they focus on countries at widely disparate levels of economic development, comparisons at this level of generality do not permit an analysis of the differences manifested among the more advanced industrial nations. The Scandinavian Social Democratic claim of welfare achievement would be trivial if the basis of comparison was the developing nations of the 'Third World'. The 'significant others' with whom the Scandinavian experience must be contrasted are the liberal-democratic capitalist states, which, to the degree that democratic socialist governments have not been in power, should, according to the Social Democratic assertion, display lower levels of welfare than exist in Scandinavia.

A recent and extremely interesting study by Harold Wilensky appears to offer a certain amount of evidence on this point. He too starts from a comparison of countries at diverse economic levels, and his conclusion from a multiple regression analysis of sixty-four nations merits quotation:

> Over the long pull, economic level is the root cause of welfare-state development, but its effects are felt chiefly through demographic changes of the past century and the momentum of the programs themselves, once established. With modernization, birth rates declined, and the proportion of the aged thereby increased. This increased importance of the aged, coupled with the declining economic value of children, in turn exerted pressure for welfare spending. Once the programs were established they matured, everywhere moving towards wider coverage and higher benefits. Social security growth begins as a natural accompaniment of economic growth and its demographic outcomes; it is hastened by the interplay of political elite perceptions, mass pressures, and welfare bureaucracies (Wilensky, 1975, p. 47).

However, Wilensky also presents a comparison of twenty-two advanced nations (including all three Scandinavian countries), and whilst he suggests that the diversity of welfare performance they manifest is partly a consequence of varied social structures, the subsequent discussion of the advanced nations still points to the level of economic development, mediated by the progressive growth of a dependent sector too old to receive a share of the national product in virtue of participation in the labour market, as the chief explanation of variation in social welfare provision.

This latter finding appears to be particularly significant in undermining the Scandinavian Social Democratic claim that political agency has been the major factor in welfare development since, in his analysis of the advanced nations, Wilensky pays special attention to the ideological variable. He devises an index of the ideological stance of governing elites in respect of a belief in 'planning for equality', comprising attitudes to social welfare provision, redistribution of wealth, economic planning and government ownership of the means of production, and another in respect of a belief in 'equality of opportunity', and finds that they *consistently add nothing* to the explanation of social security spending (Wilensky, 1975, p. 46. My italics). At the most, ideology can be regarded as a weak independent variable in explaining the diversity of welfare performance among the richer countries. Indeed, somewhat counter-intuitively, Wilensky suggests that it may well be a dependent variable in the sense that '[a] people accustomed to big spending who also like its results will develop a pro-welfare-state ideology and will more readily pay for further expansion of services, including income-equalizing benefits' (Wilensky, 1975, pp. 50-1).

However, there is one catch in the assertion that 'ideology consistently adds nothing', since the author does not provide adequate information to suggest which ideologies he has in mind. Ideologies cannot be described on a continuous spectrum of greater or lesser 'planning for equality' and 'equality of opportunity', since the important dividing lines fall *within* these categories, and specifically relate to the strategies by which an egalitarian society can be achieved. Attention has already been paid to the fact that the democratic socialist strategy is premised on the possibility of preserving a modified market mechanism, and focuses on social welfare reforms and income redistribution via taxation rather than a frontal attack on the reward system of capitalism by means of government ownership of the means of production. It is precisely this which differentiates it from the Communist or, indeed, any Marxist ideology, which reverses the order of priorities inherent in the democratic socialist strategy. But Wilensky's twenty-two advanced nations include countries with Communist, democratic socialist and non-socialist governments, and his index of 'planning for equality' conflates social welfare provision and government ownership of the means of production as interchangeable facets of a single ideological measure. Given that the seven countries in Wilensky's sample which had predominantly 'socialist' administrations in the period under investigation were Czechoslovakia, East Germany, Israel, Norway, Sweden and the USSR, it is perhaps not altogether surprising that 'ideology consistently adds nothing'. If it did, democratic socialists and Communists alike might have to reassess their ideologies.[3]

It is significant that, having relegated the role of ideology to that of a largely dependent variable as a consequence of his comparison of the advanced industrial countries of East and West, Wilensky, in his attempt to formulate structural explanations for the diversity of welfare spending of the rich countries of the West, elaborates a hypothesis which reintroduces the importance of working-class politics by the back door.[4]

> A large, strongly organized working class with high rates of participation in working-class organizations such as unions, churches, co-ops, leisure and other voluntary associations fosters pro-welfare-state ideologies and big spending (Wilensky, 1975, p. 65).

One assumes that it is only because it is a sociologist speaking that the word 'parties' does not appear in this list, and that they are included under 'other voluntary associations'. If so, it would appear that the apologists of Scandinavian Social Democracy can breathe again, since, presumably, the structural characteristics mentioned can be regarded as equivalent to the unity and integration of the labour movement, which was shown to be such a crucial feature of the development of Scandinavian Social Democratic political dominance. However, it should be noted that Wilensky's view is that '[whatever] their form, the strength of working-class-based organization is significant' (Wilensky, 1975, p. 65). It matters not whether the organisation is socialist, religious (as in the Netherlands) or linguistic (as in Belgium) in character; 'what counts is the collective push for equality' (Wilensky, 1975, p. 66). When, in the next sections I attempt to compare levels of welfare in the liberal democracies of the West, it will be necessary to bear in mind the possibility that any differences manifested may be more directly related to the organised strength of the working class than to the nature of its ideological expression.

In concluding this section several points should be noted. The reader who is acquainted with the copious Scandinavian literature on income distribution and social welfare may well wonder why no mention has been made of it. Indeed, much of this literature has been inspired by a new awakening of interest in the problems of social and economic equality, which have been a major feature of Scandinavian intellectual debate in the last decade. Each country has had major official or semi-official studies on income distribution — in the typical Scandinavian manner, commissioned by Social Democratic politicians but largely conducted by academics — and in each country Social Democrats have been shocked to find out how great is the egalitarian task still facing them.[5] Each study has led to a proliferation of research in new areas in which the goal of a humane welfare society has yet to be achieved. Virtually all this literature is relevant to a final assessment of what Social Democracy has achieved and what remains to be done. However, since it consists almost entirely of single-nation studies and inter-Scandinavian comparisons, it cannot readily be utilised in the context of a wider comparative endeavour. This being the case, it is my intention to discuss parts of this literature in a later section, having first established a framework of comparison.

The few studies which have been reviewed in this section are sufficient to reveal that it is at least as important to be agnostic in assessing the arguments of those who have compared the Scandinavian experience with other countries as it is to be sceptical about the claims of achievement made by Social Democratic ideologues. However, two very significant points did emerge. First, although a major transformation of the reward structure of capitalism is not perhaps the most immediate objective of a democratic socialist strategy, the doubts about the progress towards a more egalitarian distribution do constitute a genuine criticism of the extent of the Social Democratic achievement. This is an area in which satisfactory cross-national data is almost completely lacking, but, utilising the Scandinavian literature mentioned above, I shall at least attempt to present the main features of income distribution in Scandinavia in such a way that the reader can make a comparison with his own country. Second, it was argued that the most important criterion of Social Democratic achievement was the nature and extent of welfare state reforms. In this context, what is significant about Wilensky's study, despite its deficiencies, is that it shows that welfare reforms may have many explanations apart from direct political agency. In the next sections, I shall attempt to show not only that the level of welfare state provision in Scandinavia is exceptionally high, but also that *the most satisfactory explanation* lies in the political ascendancy of Social Democratic parties in those countries.

2.2 Devising a measure of welfare state provision

The most fundamental problem in comparisons of welfare state provision is obtaining adequate cross-national data. In so far as the researcher's conceptualisation of his field of investigation leads him to ask specific questions, the chances are extremely high that the data required to answer them will either not exist at all or will be in a form which makes comparison difficult. The basic reason lies in the fact that statistical information is generally prepared for the use of policy-makers in a par- ticular nation, and the categories utilised are, not unnaturally, those deemed most suitable in light of the particular characteristics and prob- lems of that nation. International agencies, such as the United Nations, UNESCO and OECD, have exerted a growing pressure for uniform statistical measures and this has led to great improvements in the post- war decades, but the frequency of explanatory footnotes in the statisti- cal tables provided by such agencies testifies to the difficulties involved. The information provided by international bodies is also generally of the most basic kind, since data which have major costs attached to their collection may only exist for a selection of countries, and, then, proba- bly in a non-comparable form. Occasionally, international agencies provide non-routine studies of particular problem-areas, but the infor- mation which results offers only a cross-sectional snapshot of reality at a particular time. Such information dates rapidly. It should also be noted that all information stemming from official sources is subject to the ability and willingness of the authorities to publish accurate data. Finally, when one takes into account the probability that the questions which are of interest to academic researchers will not necessarily be those which are of immediate concern to policy-makers, it will readily be appreciated that the situation in respect of adequate data for com- parative social policy investigation is generally poor, nasty, brutish and fragmentary.

This situation frequently forces the researcher into a 'second best' strategy in which he assembles the best evidence available, rather than pursuing the hopeless search for the optimum data for his specific purposes. It should be pointed out that the 'second best' strategy is, in reality, the only strategy that is possible under the circumstances, and to criticise its use *per se* is to reject the possibility of a comparative study of anything but the most trivial matters. This comparative strategy generally involves one or a combination of the following features:

(1) Inference from indicators which are more or less directly related to the subject under investigation. In other words, where the necessary data is unavailable, one attempts to find information which resembles it as closely as possible. A judgment on the validity of the resulting comparison is a consequence of the degree to which that inference seems warranted by our knowledge of the phenomena under investigation. To give a single example, Parkin argues that '[the] proportion of working-class youths in the full-time student population is perhaps the best single index of the openness of the educational system as a whole' (Parkin, 1971, p. 111). However, presumably because such an index is not readily available, he uses a measure of the percentage of grammar school and university students of working-class origin as an alternative indicator. The validity of this inference seems somewhat dubious in light of our knowledge of the very considerable variations between nations in respect of the percentage of the population attending grammar schools and universities. Whether or not this particular inference is justified, it should be emphasised that the problem of inference is inherent in all, and not merely comparative, research to the degree that words or symbols are used as a signification for events in the real world.[6]

(2) Information with less than optimum coverage. In other words, because information is fragmentary, one attempts to make a case with what is available. Whether the resulting comparison is worthwhile depends entirely on how representative is the data on which it is based. A hypothetical example of unrepresentative coverage would be a study of the relationship between educational opportunity and ideology in advanced nations which restricted its sample to the countries of Western Europe. Whereas, within Western Europe, there appears to be a relatively strong connection between a democratic socialist ideology and enhanced educational opportunity, a glance at Eastern Europe or North America shows that other ideologies may be conducive to similar results. Any comparative study necessarily works within certain limiting parameters — developing nations, welfare states, Communist polities, etc. — but within them the objective must always be to obtain maximum coverage in order to avoid the danger that the conclusions will be vitiated by an unrepresentative sample.

(3) Information which fails to reflect the contemporary situation.

In other words, where up-to-date information cannot be elicited, one relies on data which describes past states. The validity of such a procedure depends on the likelihood of change in the intervening period. In so far as one is investigating the claim that political action can alter the outcomes of social policy, it is important to utilise information that reflects the contemporary situation as nearly as possible. For example, Wilensky's data-set reflects trends in social security spending between 1949 and 1966. There can be no criticism of the fact that the data reflect a situation which existed some eight or nine years before Wilensky's book was published, since 1966 was the last year for which complete information existed at the time he wrote. The problem, however, is indicated by the knowledge that we now have of the dramatic growth of social security spending in certain countries in the intervening period. Thus, in the period 1966-73, the percentage of Gross National Product devoted by each of the Scandinavian countries to social security increased by more than a half.[7] It is not that conclusions reached on 1966 data are erroneous, it is rather that they many not be applicable today.

In the choice of a data-base for a comparative investigation there is a certain degree of trade-off between the features of the comparative strategy that have been discussed. It is possible to choose the data which seem most directly related to one's subject-matter and accept as a consequence that coverage must be restricted. Similar trade-offs are possible between direct relevance and contemporary information and between coverage and contemporaneousness. In my view, the best trade-off is that which maximises coverage and contemporary information at a minimum cost in direct relevance. This is because inference, whether implicit or explicit, is open to rational appraisal, whereas data which cannot be inspected is not open to any form of appraisal. It is better to have a true idea of the approximate nature of reality than to have an approximate idea of the true nature of reality.

In what follows, I intend to make my inferences wholly explicit, so that the reader who disagrees with me will know why that is the case before he inspects the data. The data itself will have the widest possible coverage of those economically advanced and liberal-democratic nations of the West to which Scandinavian Social Democrats normally compare their countries. Moreover, the data will be as contemporary as is compatible with two publication timetables: the original sources and my own. More important still, it will be routinely produced data, so that the reader will be in a position to test whether my conclusions hold next year and the year after. The ability to validate my conclusions should be enhanced in so far as the statistical manipulation of the data has been kept to a bare minimum. It involves nothing fundamentally more complicated than addition, long division and a little spare time.

There would be little point in claiming an outstanding achievement in welfare reform which was only discernible by means of computer analysis.

I have previously argued that the most important criterion of achievement of the democratic socialist parties is their capacity to effect welfare state reforms. It was suggested that the Social Democratic strategy had involved an attempt to restrict the operation of the market in certain areas and, in particular, to make certain goods objects of public rather than private consumption and to reallocate benefits from wage earners to those incapable of receiving remuneration through the labour market. This is the nature of the reality that will be investigated by means of a measure of welfare state provision. This measure is itself composed of four separate indicators:

(a) The current revenue of the general government as a percentage of Gross Domestic Product.

This indicator shows the extent to which central and local government, rather than the market mechanism, is the basic arbiter of the distribution of national resources. General government revenue accrues largely from various types of taxation and social security contribution, and is disbursed under headings which include the purchase of goods and services for civil and military purposes, interest on public debt, subsidies and transfers to households. The great virtues of general government revenue as an indicator of welfare state provision are that it includes both public consumption and transfers to the non-productive sector, and is, at the same time, a recognisably socialist measure of achievement. Although socialists are by no means agreed on the strategy best suited to removing the ills of capitalism, all are united in seeing one of capitalism's most serious symptoms in the contrast between the private affluence of a small minority and the public squalor of the community as a whole. Although a high level of national resources under public control may not be a sufficient condition of socialist achievement, it is a necessary condition.

However, despite these virtues, it would be absurd to pretend that this indicator does more than capture an approximation of the reality of welfare state provision. There are several reasons why this should be so. General government revenue covers all those areas in which the operation of the market is restricted, but the problem is that the market mechanism may be supplanted for purposes other than welfare state reform. Thus, general government revenue might be regarded as an inadequate indicator of welfare state provision because it is contaminated by the non-welfare uses to which it is put. The problem is one of knowing what are and what are not welfare objectives. Much government revenue is devoted to the salaries of those who staff government offices, but, while some may regard this as an essential running-cost of the modern welfare state machinery, others see it as a profligate waste on 'underproductive and overpaid papershufflers'. In theory, of course, the *democratic* socialist concedes the right of the electorate to choose what government they will, and can hardly complain too vociferously if public decision-making processes give rise to a welfare-function for the community which does not coincide with its own. In reality, this is too facile, and it is possible to identify at least one area of government spending that virtually all democratic socialists would regard as incompatible with egalitarian and welfare state objectives; namely, heavy military expenditure. Needless to say, the Scandinavian countries do not have very large defence budgets in comparative terms. Sweden and Norway spent between 2 and 3 per cent more of their Gross National Product on defence in 1970 than did Japan, Austria, Finland, Ireland and Switzerland; on the other hand, they spent nearly 5 per cent less than the United States (US Arms Control and Disarmament Agency 1972, pp. 18-21). Although these differences should be born in mind in interpreting the current revenue indicator, they do not seem sufficient to contaminate it as a measure of the *relative position* of the Scandinavian nations in respect of welfare state provision.

Another possible objection to this indicator is that it is not a true measure of the extent to which national resources are allocated according to public rather than market priorities, since, without the socialist guarantee of national ownership, the capitalist mechanism is able to subvert the processes of public decision-making by shaping the constraints under which priorities are formulated. This is, of course, the theoretical issue which divides Marxists and democratic socialists, and the only way in which one could decide it would be the use of an indicator of equality. However, it should be noted that the current revenue of the general government does capture one aspect of egalitarian distribution. In so far as governments provide services as objects of collective consumption, they do create at least a potential for individuals to have access on the basis of equal citizenship rights rather than unequal market position.

(b) Total public spending on education as a percentage of Gross National Product.

One area in which access has been progressively based on citizenship rights is education. It might, therefore, be assumed that an indicator of the extent of educational opportunity would be an additional measure of welfare state provision. This is, however, an area of much controversy. Given the well known propensity for the children of privileged groups to take up the available educational opportunities before children of working-class origin, it is possible to argue, as does Wilensky, that 'education is probably a transfer payment from the parents of the less affluent to the children of the more affluent' (Wilensky, 1975, p. 5). Moreover, as was noted previously, Scase suggests that the educational opportunity may have very little connection with social mobility, and recent evidence from Swedish sources shows that working-class children remain at a considerable disadvantage at all stages of post-primary education (Gesser and Fasth, 1973).

However, a number of important points can be advanced in favour of the use of an educational indicator. Virtually all advanced nations have devoted a greater share of national resources to education in recent years. Although the ideological incentives for such policy initiatives have not necessarily been egalitarian in character, there has, in general, been an improvement in the quantity and quality of the education experienced by working-class children. However, both initial levels of educational opportunity and rates of expansion have differed widely from country to country. Educational financing may have a net regressive impact on *current* income distribution, but the extent of regressiveness must partly depend on the rates of working-class enrolment in various types of post-primary education. Finally, there are reasons to believe that, although the expansion of educational opportunity may have little impact on social mobility, it may have long-term implications for income equalisation between those at different levels in the class hierarchy. The theories advanced by the 'human capital' school of economics have been the subject of much argument, but suffice it to say that I feel that there has not yet been an adequate refutation of the view that the demand for labour with advanced educational skills, and consequently the price it commands on the market, is at least partially determined by its supply. This view is most cogently presented by Assar Lindbeck, and it is interesting that he points to possible confirmation in recent Swedish labour market trends.

> [From] about the mid-sixties . . . B.A.s in business economics, dentists (in national service), technical college engineers and secondary school teachers have experienced a *fall* in their incomes relative to, for instance, metal workers and semi-qualified white-collar workers. . . . Thus, some narrowing of wage differentials may already have occurred between people with academic training and others from about the middle of the sixties (Lindbeck, 1975, p. 298).

If the increase in the supply of human capital produced by education can lead to an equalisation of income distribution, it becomes a crucial element in the democratic socialist argument, since it implies that education is not merely an increment to welfare, but also an instrument of egalitarian transformation of the reward structure of capitalism.

Total public spending on education has both advantages and disadvantages as a measure of educational opportunity. Its major advantages are that it constitutes a measure which shows the government's total commitment to education and that it does so in a way which is not affected by the enormous differences between types of educational system. This latter was the decisive reason for preferring it to other possible indicators. The disadvantage which is most crucial to the argument that educational effort has a potentially equalising effect is that this indicator does not show the differences between nations in access to post-primary education. With the ritual warning about the non-comparability of different categorisations of secondary and tertiary levels of education, I present the relevant UNESCO data for 1973 educational enrolments for all the countries to which the measure of welfare state provision will be applied.

Table 2.1 Gross enrolment ratios in education at the second and third levels in twenty-five nations

Country	Level 2	Level 3	Country	Level 2	Level 3
Australia	71	19.01*	Luxembourg	58	1.99†
Austria	90	15.92	Netherlands	100	20.89*
Belgium	79	20.56	New Zealand	69	27.95
Canada	98	35.08	*Norway*	92	20.79
Denmark	84	27.04	Portugal	81	9.05
Finland	107 [*sic*]	15.68	Spain	68	10.43
France	86	17.27	*Sweden*	70	20.09
Germany F.R.	70	18.05	Switzerland	64	12.39
Greece	76	13.56	Turkey	30	5.83
Iceland	na	na	United Kingdom	76*	15.00*
Ireland	61	13.51	United States	91	51.53
Italy	68	21.52	Yugoslavia	49*	16.77*
Japan	94	18.52*			

Source: *Unesco Statistical Yearbook 1975*, pp. 84–119.
*1972 data.
†University enrolment data in Luxembourg reflect the country's dependence on foreign centres of learning.

Whilst enrolment at the tertiary level is probably a reasonably comparable measure of access to high education, the data for the secondary level are almost entirely a reflection of the national educational structure and the age of transition from primary to secondary education. A better, although for similar reasons, not perfect, indicator would be enrolment rates for children in secondary education at a specified age level. The few figures that I can provide show that Sweden's relatively low rate of secondary enrolment as demonstrated in Table 2.1 is not manifested in low rates among the older age groups in secondary education.

Table 2.2 Full-time enrolment rates for children aged 15-18 as a percentage of the total age group

Country and date	enrolment %	Country and date	enrolment %
Austria (1969)	31.9	Netherlands (1970)	68.9
Belgium (1966)	54.2	*Norway* (1970)	68.9
Denmark (1970)	51.7	*Sweden* (1972)	68.1
Germany F.R. (1969)	30.5	United Kingdom (1970)	39.4

Source: OECD, *The Educational Situation in OECD Countries,* 1974, p. 27.

Table 2.2 makes it quite clear that Germany and Austria are the laggards in the provision of educational opportunities, whilst Norway, Sweden and Denmark are amongst the European leaders. Tables 2.1 and 2.2 have been provided to offer the reader some perspective on the potential equalising impact of education, in addition to the index of educational spending which comprises a part of the measure of welfare state provision.

(c) Infant mortality (Deaths in first year per 1,000 live births).
A high level, and egalitarian distribution, of health care is clearly an important aspect of welfare state provision. The value of the infant mortality indicator has been outlined by Bruce Russett.

Quite possibly the infant mortality rate gives the best overall measure of national health that we have. Almost certainly these data are more reliable, and more comparable, than for example the series on physicians or hospitals per 100,000. Of course they measure directly only the facilities available to the very young, but they seem to be highly correlated with the general level of medical care and well-being, *especially as distributed throughout subsectors of the population.* Part of the reason is that a relatively modest expenditure on medical care can reduce a very high infant mortality rate (over 200 per 1,000) to a moderate one (around 75). Quite substantial additional expenditure may be necessary, however, to reduce the rate from 50 to 30. Thus a modest amount of medical care, spread fairly evenly throughout a population, may be expected to result in a moderate infant mortality rate. But the same amount of money, heavily concentrated, will produce a low rate for a small minority of the population and leave a high infant mortality rate for the great majority — and consequently a rather high mean rate (Russett et al., 1964, p. 199. My italics).

There is only one further point that should be emphasised in the context of the comparison I am trying to make. Infant mortality seems to be an excellent measure of the equality of health provision, but it is not necessarily a measure of deliberate government intervention to procure that goal. The health coverage required to procure a low infant mortality rate may be financed from either public or private sources, and there are a few countries with high government spending and a high infant mortality rate or low government spending and low infant mortality.[8] Thus, the indicator of infant mortality should not be seen as measuring merely an aspect of government expenditure, but rather as an index of society's care for the weak. If some countries, with relatively low levels of general government revenue, have a higher general level of health care than countries with much higher levels of public spending, that can hardly be regarded as to their detriment. From a welfare point of view, it is not impossible that a *caring* capitalist state is better than an *uncaring* socialist one!

(d) Gross Domestic Product per capita in United States dollars.

This indicator is in many ways the most controversial of the four that make up my measure of welfare state provision. It is controversial because it cannot be justified in terms of socialist theory or egalitarian practice. It is simply a measure of the share that would accrue to each individual if the Gross Domestic Product *were divided equally*. As such, it is a measure of national wealth and not of national, much less individual, welfare, However, it does have important welfare implications. Of the three indicators previously discussed, only the level of infant mortality is a direct measure of the quantity and quality of welfare *output*. Both the revenue and education indicators are measures of welfare *effort*.[9] Although they provide a basis for a comparison of who tries hardest, they offer no indication of who succeeds best. Percentages of Gross Domestic Product offer little information about which countries have the best ratios of doctors to patients, the highest pensions, the smallest number of children per classroom, and all the other host of issues which concern policy-makers and their critics in any particular country. This is my justification for including *per capita* Gross Domestic Product as a separate indicator of welfare state provision. By itself it provides no direct information about welfare but, together with other indicators, it gives an approximation of the reality of the standards of welfare which are available to the working class in each of the twenty-five countries compared.

In concluding this discussion of my four indicators of welfare state provision, I wish to reiterate two points. First, even taking all four indicators together, I do not claim that they offer more than an approximation of the reality of welfare state provision. Whether even that claim is accepted will depend on the extent to which the reader is willing to accept, in whole or part, the various inferences from data to reality which have been introduced throughout the discussion. For the reader who is only willing to concede a part of my case, I shall provide separate measures for each variable before combining them in a single index, thus enabling him to arrive at his own assessment of comparative welfare state performance. Furthermore, I shall combine the data in two stages so that it is possible to judge the extent to which the GDP per capita variable contaminates the final index. This is particularly important, since it will have been noticed that my assertion that there is little connection between welfare effort and welfare output, involves an implicit rejection of the primacy of economic development as the major explanation of welfare state provision among the advanced nations. Since GDP *per capita* is the most frequently used measurement of the level of economic development, that indicator must be kept separate from the others until the relationship between them has been discussed. That nothing more than an approximation of reality is intended will be underlined by the fact that I have made no attempt to weight the four variables included in my measure of welfare state coverage. The resulting index is no more than a somewhat sophisticated rank ordering of twenty-five nations, taking some account of the degree of dispersion manifested on each indicator, but absolutely none of normality or skewness of distribution.

My second point relates to the nature of the reality which I am attempting to approximate. Although I have tried throughout this discussion to show that the indicators — or rather the first three of them — have a relevance to socialist concepts of egalitarianism, I do not claim that they constitute a measure of equality. Rather, the reality I attempt to capture is of a state which intervenes to limit private avarice and promote public welfare. However, that reality does have implications for equality, as T. H. Marshall pointed out:

The extension of the social services is not primarily a means of equalising incomes. In some cases it may, in others it may not. The question is relatively unimportant; it belongs to a different department of social policy. What matters is that there is a general enrichment of the concrete substance of civilised life, a general reduction of risk and insecurity, an equalisation between the more and less fortunate at all levels — between the healthy and the sick, the employed and the unemployed, the old and the active, the bachelor and the father of a large family. Equalisation is not so much between classes as between individuals within a population which is treated for this purpose as though it were one class. Equality of status is more important than equality of income (Marshall, 1950, p. 56).

Equality, thus conceived, is by no means an exclusively socialist virtue, but, as I hope to show, democratic socialists in Scandinavia have been amongst its most successful practitioners.

2.3 The data and an interpretation

The data for each indicator are presented in Table 2.3. Data for indicators I, III and IV are from the OECD's international comparison of basic statistics which is provided as an annex to the organisation's annual economic surveys for member nations. The source for indicator II is the *Unesco Statistical Yearbook 1975*. Although it is not my intention to present any form of analysis of rates of change, it will be noted that the indicators are ideally suited as sources of time-series data. OECD data are for 1974 and UNESCO data for 1973. In parenthesis, I have provided the rank order for each variable. This facilitates comprehension of each series of data and, simultaneously, constitutes the simplest available index of each nation's performance with regard to a particular indicator.

The nations covered are those for which information is provided by the OECD on an annual basis. They include the vast majority of economically advanced and liberal-democracies of the West. They also include a number of nations which, measured on one or several indicators, are at a rather lower level of economic and social development. This has been indicated by dividing Table 2.3 into two parts: Part 1 covers seventeen advanced countries and Part 2 includes eight somewhat less-advanced nations. The major anomaly is my inclusion of Japan in Part 2. Whereas the criterion for inclusion in Part 2 was otherwise a GDP *per capita* of less than $3,000 per annum, the reason in Japan's case was the low level of general government revenue.

The justification for an arbitrary division between advanced and less advanced nations, and for the exclusion of Japan from Part 1, becomes evident in the context of the indices presented in Table 2.4. My objective is to provide indices demonstrating the variation between the welfare performance of advanced nations. However, to base such indices on the extreme low values manifested by some of the less advanced nations, or of Japan in respect to government spending, would obscure the differences between the advanced nations. Thus, to give the example which emerges most dramatically from even a cursory examination of Table 2.4,

Table 2.3 Values and rank orders of four indicators of welfare for OECD
countries[1]

Countries	Current revenue of general government as % of GDP[2] I	Public spending on education as % of GNP[3] II	Deaths in first year per 1,000 live births[4] III	GDP *per capita* in US dollars[5] IV
Part 1:	1974	1973	1974	1974
Australia	28.9 (18)	5.0 (18)	16.1 (13)	5877 (9)
Austria	38.4 (11)	5.1 (16)	23.5 (21)	4372 (16)
Belgium	37.9 (12)	5.1 (16)	16.2 (14)	5466 (11)
Canada	38.6 (10)	8.0 (1)	16.8*(16)	6464 (5)
Denmark	47.4 (4)	7.5 (5)	12.0†(7)	6026 (7)
Finland	38.7 (9)	6.3 (7)	10.2 (3)	4712 (14)
France	38.9 (8)	5.3 (13)	12.0 (7)	5061 (13)
Germany	41.4 (6)	4.1 (22)	21.9 (19)	6195 (6)
Iceland	na	4.8 (19)	9.6*(1)	6465 (4)
Luxembourg	44.3 (5)	5.6 (10)	13.5†(10)	5987 (8)
Netherlands	51.4 (1)	7.8*(2)	11.2 (6)	5109 (12)
New Zealand	na	5.2 (15)	15.5 (12)	4388 (15)
Norway	48.5 (3)	7.8 (2)	10.4 (4)	5487 (10)
Sweden	49.4 (2)	7.7 (4)	9.6 (1)	6878 (2)
Switzerland	35.8 (13)	4.7 (20)	12.8*(9)	7340 (1)
United Kingdom	40.0 (7)	6.3 (7)	16.7 (15)	3371 (18)
United States	30.2*(17)	6.7 (6)	17.6*(17)	6660 (3)
Part 2:				
Greece	24.2 (21)	1.6 (25)	23.9 (22)	2139 (22)
Ireland	35.1*(14)	5.3 (13)	17.8*(18)	2180 21)
Italy	32.6 (15)	5.4 (12)	22.6 (20)	2706 (19)
Japan	24.7 (20)	4.3 (21)	10.8 (5)	4152 (17)
Portugal	23.0 (23)	2.1 (23)	44.8*(23)	1517 (23)
Spain	23.1 (22)	2.1 (23)	13.6 (11)	2446 (20)
Turkey	27.5 (19)	5.6 (10)	153.0††(25)	748 (25)
Yugoslavia	31.5 (16)	6.0 (9)	45.0 (24)	1315 (24)

[1] Figures in brackets indicate rank order in series.
[2] OECD, 1977 (Basic Statistics: International Comparisons).
[3] *Unesco Statistical Yearbook 1975*, pp. 372-91.
[4] Source as 2 above.
[5] Source as 2 above.
*1973.   †1972.   ††1967.

Table 2.4 Selected comparisons of welfare for OECD countries

Countries	Index of government revenue[1] — I	Index of educational spending[2] — II	Index of infant mortality[3] — III	Index of pure welfare — I-III	Index of GDP *per capita*[4] — IV	Index of welfare state provision — I-IV
Sweden	91	92	100	94	88	93
Norway	87	95	94	92	62	85
Netherlands	100	95	88	94	44	82
Denmark	82	87	83	84	67	80
Canada	43	100	48	64	80	68
Luxembourg	68	38	72	60	66	61
Finland	44	56	96	65	34	58
Switzerland	31	15	77	41	100	56
France	44	31	83	53	43	50
United States	6	67	42	38	83	50
Belgium	40	26	53	40	53	43
United Kingdom	49	56	49	51	0	39
Germany	56	0	17	24	71	36
Australia	0	23	53	25	63	35
Japan	−19	5	91*	26	20	24
Austria	42	26	0	22	25	23
Ireland	28	31	41	33	−30	18
Italy	16	33	6	18	−17	10
Spain	−26	−51	71*	−2	−23	−7
Greece	−21	−64	−3	−30	−31	−30
Yugoslavia	12	49	−155	−31	−52	−37
Portugal	−26	−51	−153	−77	−47	−69
Turkey	−6	38	−931	−300	−66	−241
Iceland	na	8	100	−	78	−
New Zealand	na	28	58	−	26	−

Sources: calculated from data in Table 2.3.

[1] $\dfrac{(x_i - \text{Min}) \times 100}{\text{Max} - \text{Min}} = \text{Index}$

Where x_i = General government revenue as a percentage of GDP.

[2] Index calculated as in 1.

Where x_i = Public spending on education as a percentage of GNP.

[3] $\dfrac{(\text{Max} - x_i) \times 100}{\text{Max} - \text{Min}} = \text{Index}$

Where x_i = Deaths in first year per 1,000 live births.

[4] Index calculated as in 1.

Where x_i = GDP *per capita*.

In all indices, Maximum (Max) and Minimum (Min) figures are calculated from Part 1 of Table 2.3.   *See note 8 to this chapter.

my interest is less in the fact that all advanced nations have much lower infant mortality rates than Turkey, but rather in the reasons why a rich country like West Germany should have such a low level of health coverage when compared with a much poorer country like Finland. In consequence, although I have included all the countries for which there is complete data, the indices constructed for each of the four indicators are measures which are based on the degree of variation *between the advanced nations included in Part 1.* Whilst the range of variation between these countries is expressed on a scale from 0-100, nations which fall below the lowest magnitude of the countries in Part 1 are given negative values which express the degree of shortfall in relation to the level of the advanced nations. It should be emphasised that the actual index numbers for the advanced countries give no indication of absolute level of welfare, but only the level relative to other advanced countries. Thus an index of 0 means that a country has the lowest value of the seventeen included in Part 1, and index of 100 means that it has the highest level, and an index of 50 indicates that it falls exactly at the mid-point in the distribution between highest and lowest.

In addition to providing indices which reflect variation in the four indicators discussed in the previous section, I have constructed two additional indices. The first I call the *Index of Pure Welfare* — pure in the sense that it does not include a measure of national wealth. This index is arrived at by summing the values for each country on indices I-III and dividing by three. The second is the *Index of Welfare State Provision,* and for all the reasons already suggested, I consider it a measurement of the approximate degree of welfare achievement. It is constructed by summing the values for each country on indices I-IV and dividing by four. Summing the indices derived from the four variables does not necessarily guarantee that they will receive equal weighting, since that also depends on the range of dispersion for each variable. In general, the degree of dispersion on each variable manifested by the countries included in Part 1 of Table 2.3 is remarkably similar.[10] To the extent that there is any bias, it is slightly in favour of government revenue and public spending on education. In terms of a measure of welfare state provision, that may not altogether be a bad thing.

It will be noted that my division of Table 2.3 into two parts concedes an important aspect of the hypothesis that welfare is largely determined by the level of economic development. In general, an inspection of the raw data and rank orders occurring in Part 2 shows that very low levels of GDP *per capita* go with very low levels on the other indicators. Apart from the somewhat anomalous infant mortality rates of Japan and Spain (see note 8), the most significant divergence from that pattern seems to be Yugoslavia, whose government revenue and educational spending are rather higher than might be expected on the basis of the GDP *per capita* indicator. It will not go unnoticed that there is a significant ideological difference between Yugoslavia and the other nations represented in Part 2.

However, amongst the advanced nations in Part 1, there is anything but a clear relationship between economic development and welfare.

Table 2.5 Rank orders of, and differences between, index scores for GDP *per capita* and Pure Welfare for fifteen advanced nations

Countries	Rank order for GDP *per capita* A	Rank order for Pure Welfare B	Difference in index scores A-B
Switzerland	1	10	−59
Sweden	2	1	+6
United States	3	12	−45
Canada	4	6	−16
Germany	5	14	−47
Denmark	6	4	+17
Luxembourg	7	7	−6
Australia	8	13	−38
Norway	9	3	+30
Belgium	10	11	−13
Netherlands	11	1	+50
France	12	8	+10
Finland	13	5	+31
Austria	14	15	−3
United Kingdom	15	9	+51

This can most easily be seen by comparing the performance of these countries on the Index of GDP *per capita* and the composite Index of Pure Welfare. Table 2.5 shows the rank order of the fifteen nations in Part A for which there is complete data in respect of both indices, and gives a measure of the extent of the difference between the two index values. There appears to be a virtually random relationship between the two rank orders, and the differences between the values on the two indices are far too great to be readily compatible with the hypothesis that there is a direct connection between economic development and the level of welfare. Switzerland, the United States, West Germany and Australia stand out as countries whose level of welfare is markedly lower than their degree of economic development. The United Kingdom, the Netherlands, Finland and Norway all show a far better welfare performance than one would expect on the basis of GDP *per capita*. I would readily concede that there may a minimum threshold of economic development which permits a nation to devote a substantial proportion of its resources to welfare, but once such a threshold has been reached a purely economic explanation of the differences between the welfare performance of advanced nations is wholly inadequate.

Before leaving Table 2.5, it should be noted that it gives some support to a structural hypothesis offered by Wilensky as a partial explanation of the diversity of social security provision among the rich countries. He suggests that the centralisation of government is likely to foster high welfare spending, and shows that the federal states of Australia, Canada, Switzerland and the United States are laggards in respect of the percentage of GNP devoted to social security (Wilensky, 1975, p. 56). Although my Index of Pure Welfare covers a much wider spectrum of welfare provision than does a measure of social security spending, it also shows that the four countries with the greatest gap between welfare achievement and economic development are federal states; namely, Australia, Switzerland, the United States *and West Germany*. Canada remains a laggard, but to a much lesser degree. Despite this change in order of welfare performance from one measure to another, the two sets of findings provide complementary evidence of the serious impediment that a decentralised political structure represents for political groups pursuing welfare reform.

However, it is very significant that West Germany, which together with Austria was at the very top of Wilensky's league of social security spending, falls again together with Austria to the very bottom of the league in respect of the Index of Pure Welfare for the advanced nations. It could be argued that this massive discrepancy casts doubt on the validity of my Index of Pure Welfare, but I would claim categorically that it proves the inadequacy of social security spending as an accurate measure of welfare. Left-wing socialists frequently point to the German and Austrian social security schemes as evidence of the first beginnings of the capitalist state's attempt to buy off the radicalism of the working class, and empirically minded social scientists use the nineteenth-century origins of these schemes to argue that welfare state provision has a momentum of its own, but both are inclined to overlook their most crucial feature — that they are 'mainly of a social insurance character' (Kaim-Caudle, 1973, p. 308). Thus, the German and Austrian high percentages of GNP devoted to social security spending conceal markedly less egalitarian welfare systems than those of Britain and Scandinavia which, until recently, have tended to emphasise the provision of flat-rate social security benefits.[11] If social security spending really was an accurate index of the approximate reality of welfare state provision, one might expect it to be a reasonably good predictor of health coverage and educational opportunity. In fact, Table 2.3 shows that Germany and Austria have the highest infant mortality rates amongst the advanced countries, and amongst the lowest levels of educational spending. Tables 2.1 and 2.2 confirm these countries' low degree of access to post-primary education. The seeming anomaly of Germany and Austria's very different positions on social security and other indicators of welfare is much less surprising when it is understood that social security in these countries was never a reflection of political egalitarianism. I have made it clear that my indices of welfare cannot be regarded as measures of egalitarian welfare coverage, but it seems they give a rather better indication of that aspect than does the level of social security spending.

Turning now to the substance of the comparison of welfare levels in Scandinavia and the other advanced nations, Table 2.4 makes it quite apparent that the three Scandinavian countries *plus* the Netherlands are in a league of their own in respect of the level of welfare provision. Taking all twenty-five countries as the basis for comparison, these countries occupy the four top positions in regard to the percentage of GDP disbursed by the general government, four out of five of the top positions in regard to public spending on education and four out of seven in regard to health care. The consequence of this consistency is that there is a very wide gap between these countries and the rest on the composite Index of Pure Welfare. The one index on which the four countries differ appreciably is that for GDP *per capita*, but even when that variable is included in the final Index of Welfare State Provision, the gap remains very considerable. Thus, there does seem to be clear evidence, in respect of welfare state provision at least, that the Scandinavian Social Democratic claim that 'we're far ahead compared to other countries' is justified. With the single exception of the Netherlands, no other advanced countries manifest anything like the same consistently high levels of welfare effort and output.

However, the single exception of the Netherlands is extremely significant in providing a perspective from which to assess the link between Scandinavian Social Democratic dominance and a high level of welfare state provision. That such a link exists seems apparent given that the argument from economic development demonstrably fails to explain the variation among the advanced nations. In the absence of impersonal economic force determining the *precise* nature of social reality, it is necessary to attribute certain features of that reality to deliberate political agency. It has already been demonstrated that the dominant political actors in the Scandinavian countries during the last four decades have been the Social Democratic parties and the labour movements of which they are but a part. Of course, as in many other European countries, modern social welfare legislation in Scandinavia has antecedents in Liberal reforms of the late-nineteenth and early-twentieth centuries.[12] But the major welfare reforms in all Western countries have been a product of the last three or four decades and, in that period, the political choices made in the Scandinavian countries have been primarily the responsibility of the Social Democratic parties. In Scandinavia, Social Democratic dominance is a *sufficient condition* of a high level of welfare state provision.

The importance of the Dutch case is that it suggests that the dominance of a democratic socialist party is *not a necessary condition* for such a welfare development. The party system in the Netherlands has until recently been very different from the Scandinavian nations, although since the 1971 election there have been increasing resemblances to the Danish situation in which a democratic socialist party has a margin of dominance in a highly fragmented polity. Before the 1970s, however, the Netherlands was the model 'consociational democracy' characterised by the accommodation of deeply divided political sub-cultures which shared political responsibility in a deliberate attempt 'to counteract the immobilizing and unstabilizing effects of cultural fragmentation' (Lijphart, 1968a, p. 212). Sub-cultural divisions were at least as much religious in character as class based with two smallish Calvinist parties and a Catholic People's Party which was the largest party in the system for almost the entire period. Other organisations reflected the same cultural fragmentation and there were trade unions separately representing socialist, Catholic and Protestant workers. On the surface, the ideological divisions of politics in the Netherlands and Scandinavia seem to be poles apart; the former being divided into distinct 'pillars' representing different religious and secular attitudes and the latter manifesting a predominantly Left-Right spectrum of opinion.

Yet, only the Netherlands and the Scandinavian nations have achieved consistently high levels of welfare state in recent decades. In logic, there is no necessity for similar effects to have similar causes, but a consideration of whether, despite the surface differences, there are any fundamental common features of these societies which might explain their high levels of welfare is a precondition of understanding the factors which have led to the distinctive Scandinavian combination of Social Democratic dominance and the emergence of a humane welfare state. One possible common factor was suggested by Wilensky when he pointed to 'the collective push for equality' provided by a strongly organised working class irrespective of the nature of that organisation. This hypothesis was advanced with specific reference to the Netherlands and the caveat was intended to cover the religious fragmentation of the trade unions. However, according to Lijphart, only 'about 40 per cent of Dutch workers are union members' (Lijphart, 1968b, p. 36), and this indicates a degree of working-class organisation very considerably lower than in any of the Scandinavian countries.[13]

Although the strength of working-class organisations seems an inadequate explanation of the similar levels of welfare state provision manifested in the Netherlands and Scandinavia, it does suggest an alternative hypothesis. In polities which are divided on a Left-Right continuum, the strength of working-class organisations is likely to be inversely related to the strength of the political Right. But in a country like the Netherlands this need not necessarily be so. Given the importance of religious parties which cut across class boundaries, the political Right may be extremely weak despite the fact that working-class organisations and parties are not dominant.

If the welfare state is seen largely in T. H. Marshall's terms as conferring 'equality of status', it is not merely in the interests of the industrial working class, but also of the vast majority of wage earners, to secure as great 'a reduction of risk and uncertainty' as possible. If it is reasonable to believe that a large portion of the middle stratum of society is willing to forego some small immediate benefits in a Rawsian attempt to 'maximise the minimum', there may be less need to push for welfare than is commonly assumed. The only stratum that has a clear interest in opposing welfare initiatives, in so far as they involve a redistribution of wealth will be that which is extremely privileged compared with the majority of the population. In absolute numbers, such a social stratum is likely to be relatively small, but its political influence will depend on the historical and structural forces which have shaped the party system. My hypothesis is that, to the degree that such forces have led to the emergence of a large and united party of the Right which can act as the political instrumentality of the privileged stratum, there will be a strong impediment to welfare. It will be noticed that this is a negative hypothesis. A large party of the Right will tend to impede welfare state provision but, in its absence, the degree of such provision will depend on the choices of those whom the people elect to govern them.

This hypothesis is tested in a very simple way in Table 2.6, which compares the rank order of fifteen advanced nations on the Index of Welfare State provision with the average strength of the major party of the Right in the period 1945-72. The fifteen countries are those for which there is complete data in Part 1 of Table 2.3. I do not wish to claim too much for this table. There are real problems in defining which is the party of the Right in some cases. In the French case, as the table makes clear, the change in political system in 1958 actually seemed to justify a change in which party was designated as the major party of the Right in the middle of the series. In Belgium, it can be argued that the Liberal Party until 1961 was 'a liberal-secular-bourgeois party' and only became 'a conservative-bourgeois party' thereafter (Hill, 1974, p. 64). Had the Christian Social Party been considered the major party

Table 2.6 Rank order on Index of Welfare State Provision and average strength of parties of the Right in fifteen nations, 1945-72

Country	Rank order of Welfare State Provision	Average % of votes 1945-72	Party
Sweden	1	14.75	Conservatives
Norway	2	17.95	Conservatives
Netherlands	3	9.97	Liberal Party
Denmark	4	17.53	Conservatives
Canada	5	34.95	Conservatives
Luxembourg	6	14.61	Democratic Party
Finland	7	15.46	National Coalition
Switzerland	8	22.3	Catholic Conservatives
France	9	23.2	Conservatives II (1945-56) Gaullists (1958-68)
United States	10	49.95	Republicans
Belgium	11	14.95	Liberal Party
United Kingdom	12	44.02	Conservatives
Germany	13	44.32	Christian Democrats
Australia	14	46.16	Liberal/Country Party
Austria	15	45.2	Peoples Party

Source: electoral data calculated from Mackie and Rose, 1974.

of the Right prior to 1961, the anomalous position of Belgium in Table 2.6 would not have occurred. Apart from Belgium, the only other anomaly in the table is the relatively high average vote for the Conservative Party in Canada. The only point that should be made in this connection is that Canada is the one country with a high score on the Index of Welfare State Provision whose relative position is almost entirely determined by its high level of educational spending. I have suggested that education is an important aspect of welfare, but it might be argued that, since educational opportunity is compatible with a wide range of ideological orientations, a more sophisticated measure of welfare state provision would use the educational indicator merely as a deflationary factor showing where educational spending was inadequate in relation to GDP *per capita*. If this were done, the only major changes in order on the two composite indices of welfare would be some upward shift for Finland and an appreciable downward shift for Canada.

Despite the two anomalies in the table, it will be broadly apparent that it is compatible with my hypothesis that large parties of the Right are a major impediment to welfare state provision. Five out of six welfare laggards have parties of the Right with an average vote of 44 per cent or more; five out of six welfare leaders have parties of the Right with an average vote of 18 per cent or less. Had the comparison been the Index of Pure Welfare and the vote for parties of the Right, the result would have been rather similar. Five out of the seven lowest nations on the Pure Welfare Index have parties of the Right which average more than 44 per cent of the vote; six out of the seven of the highest nations on the Index have parties of the Right which average less than 18 per cent of the vote. Only two countries change their positions at all radically: Switzerland which drops three places in rank order and Britain which jumps three places. Switzerland, as indeed was also the case with Belgium, cannot refute my negative hypothesis, which would be quite absurd if it were taken as implying that small parties of the Right *cause* a high level of welfare state provision.

Britain rises in rank order from twelfth to ninth place, which even then hardly makes the country a paragon of welfare state virtues. None the less, the jump is significant since it is reasonable to interpret it as a reflection of the fact that, of the five countries with very strong parties of the Right, only Britain had a democratic socialist party in power for a considerable portion of the postwar era in which the welfare state was constructed. It may have been noticed that Britain was the country which had the highest positive discrepancy between its Index of Pure Welfare and its Index of GDP *per capita* in Table 2.5. That could be argued as being an indication of the British Labour Party's relative success despite the massive impediment of a firmly entrenched Conservative Party. Britain has sometimes been considered as the country which exemplifies the politics of social class. That may not be quite the correct way to put it, but it certainly seems to be the country in which there is the greatest polarisation between a strongly organised democratic socialist labour movement and a monolithic party of the Right. That is the problem of democratic socialism in Britain and it is also the problem which confronts those who would make Britain a more humane welfare society.

Despite the few anomalies in Table 2.6, I think it is possible to conclude that the hypothesis is confirmed by the results, and that it can be argued that a weak party of the Right is a *necessary condition* of a high level of welfare state provision. In the context of my discussion of the reasons for the dominance of the Scandinavian Social Democratic parties in chapter 3, I shall lay much stress on the historical and structural factors which conditioned the weakness of parties of the Right in the Scandinavian countries. It would involve an unconscionable digression to offer a detailed discussion of the sufficient conditions for the high level of welfare state provision in the Netherlands. That a weak party of the Right is not a sufficient condition for such a development is demonstrated by the somewhat lesser welfare performance of countries like Belgium, Switzerland and Luxembourg. Lijphart suggests a possible explanation in the peculiar nature of the Dutch politics of accommodation:

> The main politically significant issues after 1917 have been social and economic. The franchise problem was settled in 1917, but other big problems remained, especially those concerning the ways of fighting the depression of the 1930s and the creation of the welfare state. Vitally important elements in the successful handling of these issues have been not only the Social and Economic Council and its predecessors, but also the mitigation of tensions on these questions by the heterogenous class composition of the Catholic and Calvinist blocs. These blocs and their political and social organizations are, like the Socialist and Liberal blocs, religiously homogenous, but, unlike the Socialists and Liberals, cut across class lines. On issues affecting class interests, the Catholics and Calvinists are not automatically united within their own ranks. Compromises must be reached first within these blocs. As a result the religious parties usually take a middle-of-the-road position, and this, in turn, has a moderating effect on the entire political system (Lijphart, 1968b, p. 118).

The cross-class heterogeneity of the Dutch religious parties is not sufficient to distinguish them from Belgium, Switzerland and Luxembourg, each of which has a major religious party. However, it may be significant that in the Dutch politics of accommodation the religious element in politics has itself until recently been divided between a large Catholic and two small Calvinist parties, whereas the religious parties in the other nations have been relatively unfragmented. In consequence, it has been harder in the Netherlands for a privileged stratum bereft of a major party of its own, to use any of the religious parties as an alternative instrumentality to secure its interests.

2.4 Dimensions of equality and welfare in Scandinavia

The discussion of welfare state provision in the previous sections has made an explicit distinction between welfare reforms — better social services, improved health care and wider educational opportunity — and egalitarian measures. The former may be conducive to the latter in the sense of conferring 'equality of status' in respect of certain basic social rights, but even this may not be the case where coverage of the population is incomplete, benefits are related exclusively to contributions, or access is effectively a function of social class position. In this context, it is highly significant that the discussion of welfare in Scandinavia during the past decade has been in terms which have eluded the difference between welfare and equality. This telescoping of concepts has not been characterised, as some cynics might suppose, by an attempt to resolve any inconsistencies between the prevailing Social Democratic ideology and the reality of inequality by defining equality to mean welfare. On the contrary, it has involved an effort to broaden the concept of welfare so that it encompasses egalitarian goals.

Starting with the studies undertaken under the auspices of the Swedish Low Income Committee, Scandinavian studies of welfare have increasingly focused on the concept of the *level-of-living*.[14] A given population's level-of-living can be seen as its distribution on a number of measures of the quality of life. In the original Swedish study, nine components of the level-of-living were measured: health, nutrition, housing, family origins and family relations, education, work and work *milieu*, economic resources, political resources and leisure and leisure time pursuits (Johansson, 1971, pp. 32-7). In subsequent studies covering each of the Scandinavian countries and Finland, there have been slight variations in the components covered, but the general objective has been similar: to present as full a picture as possible of the extent and distribution of welfare in the widest sense. The concept of equality is an inherent aspect of this research endeavour since the provision of evidence regarding the *level* of living of different sub-groups of the population involves an explicit measure of the distribution of the population in respect of each component.[15]

The use of the level-of-living concept provides a helpful means of examining the major dimensions of welfare and equality in the Scandinavian countries. Galtung and Høivik (1968) suggested that, in light of the general acceptance of egalitarian goals in these societies, welfare objectives may be operationalised as increasing the average level of all components, decreasing the dispersion of inequalities within components and the covariation of inequalities between components. Thus, welfare involves a three-dimensional effort: the quality of life should be as high as possible in all respects, equality should be the aim in every area of life and, to the degree that inequalities persist, their cumulative impact on the individual should be minimised. It is my view that egalitarian attitudes are more widely held in Scandinavia than in much of the rest of the world, but I rather doubt whether, even there, all sections of society would embrace the more radical implications of this formulation. However, as a statement of traditional socialist goals, it has much to recommend it. In this section, I will give a synoptic account of the Scandinavian countries' performance with respect to each of these dimensions of welfare and equality as a preliminary to a final assessment of Social Democracy's claim to have effected a major improvement in the condition of the working class. Since this section will not provide any systematic comparisons with non-Scandinavian nations, it is important to stress that the findings should be seen in the context of Scandinavia's outstanding level of welfare state provision compared with virtually all other advanced nations. That many egalitarian and welfare goals have yet to be achieved is not necessarily an indictment of Social Democratic rule.

Something of the high average level of the quality of life in Scandinavia has emerged from the previous section. Table 2.3 shows the level of GDP *per capita* for each country in 1974. In these terms, Sweden was the second richest country in Europe, Denmark was fourth richest and Norway was seventh richest. Today, with North Sea oil (which even the most ardent protagonist of Social Democracy could not attribute to political agency) Norway either is, or soon will be, the most affluent country in Europe. Similar findings emerge from the data on educational spending and health coverage provided in Table 2.3. If the Galbraith criterion of public affluence is taken as the indicator of the good society, the figures for general government revenue in the same table are a measure of the relative excellence of public provision in the Scandinavian countries. Although it was impossible to provide up-to-date cross-national data for social security expenditure, such data are readily available for Scandinavia. Table 2.7 summarises the percentages of Gross National Income devoted to various social security purposes. Although there are some differences between the provision offered by the different social security systems, the general picture is of transfers made from wage earners to the old, the sick and families with children.

It is also possible to show the extent to which social security provision has grown during the postwar period. Table 2.8 provides indices for the growth of social security expenditure as a percentage of Gross National Income and for the growth of social security expenditure *per capita* in terms of 1948 prices. It will be noted that, whilst the former constitutes a measure of the increase in welfare effort, the latter is a measure of welfare output taking into account the extent of economic growth, a comparison of the two indices indicates that in the decade 1950-60 Norway put in a rather greater welfare effort than either

Table 2.7 Main items of social security spending in Scandinavia as a percentage of Gross National Income, 1973

Item	Denmark	Norway	Sweden
Health care and insurance	6.63	7.28	8.33
Unemployment insurance, retraining, public works, etc.	0.74	0.30	1.20
Old age, disability, etc.	9.57	8.32	7.60
Family welfare	3.48	2.02	3.36
Other	0.58	0.68	0.41
Total social security as a percentage of Gross National Income	21.00	18.60	20.90

Source: calculated from data in *Yearbook of Nordic Statistics 1975.*

Table 2.8 Indices of growth in social security expenditure in Scandinavia as a percentage of Gross National Income and *per capita* at 1948 prices

Year	Denmark % of GNI	*per capita*	Norway % of GNI	*per capita*	Sweden % of GNI	*per capita*
1950	102	115	105	114	100	107
1960	127	180	163	219	128	181
1962	138	215	178	254	132	204
1964	138	234	190	292	147	253
1966	163	294	193	328	165	305
1968	198	359	220	404	199	388
1970	221	461	282	470	217	458
1973	249	561	310	584	255	561

Source: *Yearbook of Nordic Statistics 1975.*

Denmark or Sweden, which is a reflection of Norway's rather lower initial level of social security provision. Thereafter, both indices exhibit very similar growth trends. If Table 2.8 is contrasted with Table 1.4, which gave details of governmental composition throughout the period, it will be noted that there are few significant differences between the few bourgeois administrations and the predominantly Social Democratic governments in respect of an increasing level of welfare effort. The only important exception is the massive expansion in expenditure in Denmark between 1968-73 most of which must be attributed to the welfare efforts of a bourgeois coalition government. I have already pointed out that this abdication of the traditional non-socialist role as the chief opponent of an increasing tax burden had a major impact on the Danish party system by leading to the emergence of the anti-welfare state Progress Party. In the general context of the large and consistent increases in the level of the Scandinavian welfare effort, the similarity between bourgeois and democratic socialist administrations should be read less as evidence of the laggardly performance of the latter and more as testimony to the progressiveness of the former. This is a point to which I shall return.

Before leaving the question of the absolute level of welfare, there is one general point which should be emphasised. In socialist polemic about the relative lack of virtue of all capitalist societies, discussion of this dimension of welfare is conspicuous by its absence. It is, however, absolutely fundamental to the Scandinavian Social Democratic strategy. Socialist beliefs have always stressed egalitarian distribution of the good things of life, but part of their concern has also been that the absolute standards of the poor and the unfortunate should be improved. This latter is easier to secure when the average level of all components of the level-of-living is high. The Social Democratic strategy in this respect has been cogently expressed by Gunnar Adler-Karlsson.

> [All] the parties of the economic process have realized that the most important economic task is to make the national cake grow bigger and bigger, because then everyone can satisfy his demanding stomach with a greater piece of that common cake. When instead, there is strong fighting between the classes in that society, we believe that the cake will often crumble or be destroyed in the fight, and because of this everyone loses (Adler-Karlsson, 1969, p. 18).

This was written in the late 1960s, and since that time there has been a renewed emphasis on egalitarian aims in the Scandinavian Social Democratic parties, but even where egalitarian redistribution is the objective, it is worth remembering that there is a difference between the equality of poverty and the equality of affluence. Because of the high general level of welfare provision in Scandinavia, the poor and the unfortunate receive better medical care, more adequate pensions and enjoy access to a wider range of public services and public benefits than in the majority of capitalist societies. That may be of minor consequence to some socialist theorists, but it is conceivably of significance to the poor and the unfortunate.

Despite the fact that the democratic socialist strategy involves a rather indirect attempt to reform the inegalitarian reward structure of capitalism, such an effort has always been an important objective. The two wings of the Scandinavian labour movements have attempted to secure this objective by different means. Social Democratic administrations have instituted progressive systems of direct taxation of incomes and wealth. The trade unions, particularly in Norway and Sweden, have tried to use centralised collective bargaining to implement a solidaristic wages policy with a levelling impact as between different groups on the labour market. The technical literature on income distribution is overwhelmingly complex and cross-national comparisons fraught with great danger. Thus, the most that I can do is present a very simplified picture of the Scandinavian countries in this respect. The inadequacies of my treatment of this topic should not be consequential to an exaggeration of the level of Social Democratic achievement, since my general conclusion will be that, despite the obviously genuine attempts to procure a greater degree of income equality, the degree of success has been rather limited.

The research on level-of-living in each of the Scandinavian countries provides ample evidence of the considerable inequalities that exist in the distribution of income. My major source will, however, be a cross-national comparison of the Scandinavian countries and Finland undertaken by the Research Group for Comparative Sociology at the University of Helsinki. The data-base for this comparison was a sample survey of the population aged 15-64 in each of these countries conducted in the Spring of 1972. Although income data therefore excluded both the young and the old, the findings reported for distribution by household include the vast proportion of the former and a considerable portion of the latter. The income concept is gross income, which includes income from employment plus social security transfers, *but excludes any redistributive effects of taxation*. Table 2.9 gives information on the distribution of household incomes according to the occupational status of the head of the household.

Table 2.9 reveals that in Denmark the highest income group has a household income level which is 74 per cent higher than the average whilst the lowest group has a level which is 41 per cent lower than the average. The level of household inequality is slightly less in Sweden, and quite appreciably less in Norway. As a measure of inequality household income has both advantages and disadvantages. The most important advantage is that social class is a concept which relates to position in the social hierarchy determined by family status whereas income is a measure of the resources transferred to the individual in virtue of participation in the labour market. How significant this distinction can be is shown in the finding that in Sweden those who fall below the official low income line 'live in households where total disposable income is "only" about 20 per cent below the average for households' (Lindbeck, 1975, p. 285). The distribution of household incomes by occupational group is probably the closest approach one can make to a measure of the inequality between social classes. The data presented suggest that in each of the Scandinavian countries there are large middle strata which have similar levels of household incomes: in Denmark, the farmers, lower white-collar and skilled workers in all totalling 71 per cent of the

Table 2.9 Mean household incomes by occupational status of the head of the household as a percentage of the overall mean household income

Occupational status (Date: 1972)	Denmark		Norway		Sweden	
	mean income	% of population	mean income	% of population	mean income	% of population
farmers	107*	20	68	12	56	5
entrepreneurs	141	8	118	7	115	8
upper white-collar	174	12	143	20	162	18
lower white-collar	88	18	102	22	98	24
skilled workers	82	31	88	29	86	36
unskilled workers	59	9	69	7	66	7
no information		3		2		2

Source: Hannu Uusitalo, 1975a, p. 121.
*For reasons to do with the way in which the data was collected this figure inflates farm incomes very considerably. Uusitalo suggests that a more correct figure would be 79.

population; in Norway, lower white-collar and skilled workers totalling 51 per cent of the population; and, in Sweden, lower white-collar and skilled workers totalling 60 per cent of the population. The picture that emerges is less that of an incomes pyramid and more that of a substantial middle mass flanked by smaller groups of the rich and the poor. The size of the group of middle-income households is likely to be intensified by the incidence of taxation. Lindbeck suggests that in Sweden there has been a recent change in emphasis in income distribution policy toward the reduction of income differentials between middle-income groups, and reports findings which show that the joint impact of transfers and taxation is to reduce the 10:1 ratio of factor incomes between 100,000 and 10,000 Skr. to about 2.5:1 for corresponding groups (for families with two children and one income earner) (Lindbeck, 1975, p. 306).

The occupational distribution in Table 2.9 is also of interest in showing which groups are most affluent and which are poorest. In all the Scandinavian countries, it is the upper white-collar employees who receive the highest income, and the unskilled and, in Norway and Sweden, the farmers, who receive the lowest incomes. This distribution has significant political implications since it suggests reasons why the Scandinavian centrist parties have not been actively opposed to income redistribution efforts, and why, in particular, parties with a large agrarian clientele (the Centre parties in Norway and Sweden) have been active proponents of equality policy. The findings of the various studies of income distribution in Scandinavia have had a major impact on policymakers. Thus, to give but one example, the Norwegian parties have reached an agreement whereby farm incomes are to reach the level attained by skilled industrial workers within a five-year period. The greatest political problem which emerges from the data in Table 2.9 is the low incomes of the unskilled workers. Unlike the farmers, they have no distinctive political instrumentality of their own to press for higher living standards. Their interests are represented as an aspect of the Social Democratic egalitarian effort, but it is clear from the relative size of the unskilled and skilled groups of workers that the concerns of the latter are likely to receive the most attention. Moreover, it is precisely the unskilled and casual workers who are least organised in trade unions and are, therefore, least likely to be affected by solidaristic wage policies.

A measure of the distribution of large social groups has the disadvantage that it conceals the wide discrepancies that occur within occupational groups. Uusitalo presents an alternative way of looking at the level of economic inequality by examining the distribution of household incomes *per capita* in terms of the share received by each decile of the population. I will quote his major conclusions from this comparison of the Scandinavian countries' levels of income inequality.

The similarities between the Scandinavian countries form the major themes. . . . Gross income in all countries is distributed rather unevenly. The highest decile receives a share of total income which is typically two or even three times greater than the share it would get if the distribution were completely equal. Consequently, the lowest income decile gets only a fifth or so [sic] from the share it would get in the case of complete equality. This results in enormous income differences. For instance, income per capita is from 8 to 15 times greater in the highest income decile than in the lowest income decile. . . . [F]rom 60 to70 percent of income recipients would benefit if income were distributed completely equally, and, consequently, from 40 to 30 percent would lose. . . . The third feature revealed . . . is the distinction between the top ten percent and the bottom ninety percent. . . . [W]hen one moves from the ninth decile to the tenth, there is a clear jump. Income shares sharply increase in this category compared with the [other] increases (Uusitalo, 1975a, pp. 99-100).

If one looks at the degree of inequality in gross incomes in this way, a somewhat different picture emerges. Uusitalo's data still show a wide middle stratum (in Sweden and Norway, 50 per cent and, in Denmark, 40 per cent, of the population have gross incomes which are between one-half and one-and-one-half the national average), but the extremes of riches and poverty appear much more clearly. Again, it should be emphasised that these findings relate to gross income, and that the effects of progressive taxation have some redistributive effect in reducing the share of the top decile. Uusitalo's own conclusion is that the 'redistributive effects of the state on the distribution of income are considerable in all the Scandinavian countries', but 'of these redistributive measures taxation has less effect than do social security benefits' (Uusitalo, 1975a, p. 113). These latter benefits are, of course, already included in the concept of gross income.

The use of a measure of gross household income *per capita* demonstrates the extent of inequality in the contemporary Scandinavian societies but, at the same time, it cannot be taken as an adequate indicator of the extent to which the market mechanism determines the distribution of incomes. This is because it includes those who participate in the labour market and those who do not. The reasons for not working vary enormously. They may involve deliberate choices as in the case of housewives and students, or they may be the consequence of a variety of individual misfortunes, such as sickness, full or partial unemployment and premature retirement. Clearly, individual misfortunes of this kind have more significant welfare implications than do conscious and voluntary decisions to trade-off a somewhat higher income against the value of services performed in the home or against the future benefits accruing from higher education. However, with the exception of unemployment, the implications of non-deliberate exclusion from the labour market are not so much concerned with altering the reward structure of capitalism as they are with extending still further the level of welfare state provision. Whatever the reasons for non-participation in the labour market, studies of income inequality in Scandinavia have generally shown *that about half the degree of inequality can be explained in terms of work volume rather than differential wage levels* (see Holmberg, 1970 and Uusitalo, 1975a, pp.162-7). It is this fact, together with the importance of the household as the unit which determines the level-of-living of its members, which casts serious doubt on Parkin's contention that 'the distribution of occupational income gives us perhaps the best overall view of the reward structure'.

It is much less easy to come to firm conclusions about the level of equality of incomes in Scandinavia than it was to assess the level of welfare state provision. Cross-national comparisons have generally been based on income from employment or the ratio of incomes from different types of employment. For the reasons stated above, income from occupational employment is not necessarily the best measure of inequalities stemming from the reward structure of capitalism. Moreover, such comparisons tend to be misleading to the extent that they necessarily fail to reflect differences in the composition of the workforce. To suggest one relevant example, Sweden has a very high rate of female labour market participation and, although wage-rate differentiation is probably rather less than in many countries, women do tend to earn less both because of overrepresentation in low-wage industries and because of a greater propensity to do part-time work. Thus, the effect of a higher rate of female labour market participation in Sweden will be to make the distribution of incomes from employment appear more inegalitarian compared with other countries whilst, simultaneously, increasing the degree of equality of gross income *per capita* within Sweden. Similarly, a failure to consider the size of occupational groups whose income ratios are being contrasted frequently vitiates the value of the findings reported in studies which use this particular measure of inequality. Having made the point that cross-national comparisons of income distribution should be viewed with a certain reserve, it is necessary to concur with Parkin that the comparisons which have been made show no significant differences between the distribution of income from employment and income ratios in Scandinavia and the general pattern found elsewhere in Western Europe.[16] Moreover, although data on the distribution of wealth is, if anything, less reliable than that on income from employment, there seems every reason to conclude that wealth in Scandinavia, as elsewhere in Western Europe, is considerably less evenly distributed than income.

These negative findings together with the picture of household incomes illustrated by Uusitalo's research do not suggest that Scandinavian Social Democracy has had more than limited success in its redistributional objectives. This does not mean that redistribution does not take place, but rather that, despite the creation of a broad middle stratum, there remains a deep gulf separating the rich and the poor. Moreover, it is probably correct to conclude that it is the impact of welfare state provision rather than either taxation or wage-levelling efforts by the trade unions which constitutes the most important element in the redistribution that does occur. This is a natural consequence of the fact that a substantial proportion of income inequality stems from individual misfortune and not from the agency of market forces. To the degree that low income is not a concomitant of unequal rewards from employment, it is somewhat more amenable to amelioration via social transfer payments operating as a kind of negative income tax.[17] Until recently at least, there has been less evidence to suggest that the Social Democratic strategy can have an appreciable effect on changing the reward structure that results from the operation of the market mechanism. Although for certain periods a solidaristic wages policy can lessen pre-tax differentials *between* different groups of workers, wage-drift has a strong tendency to reassert the advantage of groups in high demand. There may be some tendency for changes in the distribution of human capital to have long-term effects in lessening the differentiation between white-collar and skilled workers, but, for the most part, these groups are already in the broad middle mass and the real equality problem lies in the gross differences between the top income decile and the rest.

The gap between those who receive very high incomes or possess considerable wealth and the rest of society might aptly be described as the 'unpleasant face of Social Democracy'. The Social Democratic strategy has, hitherto, been predicated on a fundamental compromise with capitalism, permitting a small minority to reap great rewards from the ownership of capital on the condition that labour received its share of increased productivity and the government obtained the resources required to ensure that certain basic social rights were available to all irrespective of their position in the economic hierarchy. To some degree, such a strategy has even been compatible with a declining share in the profit share of national income but, clearly, it is inherent in the nature of the compromise that the owners of capital retain much of their economic privilege. Thus, the gap between the top decile and the rest is built into the very fabric of the political and economic system.

The compromise on which the Social Democratic strategy rests can be perfectly explicit — indeed, it is difficult to imagine it being more explicit than in the quotation from Gunnar Adler-Karlsson cited earlier in this section — without Social Democracy abandoning its redistributive objectives. To alleviate the condition of the unfortunate and to create a wide middle stratum, including the mass of the industrial working class, is redistributive in terms of a comparison with the past ('we're far ahead compared to what Sweden looked like thirty or forty years ago'). However, the viability of the compromise depends on two crucial preconditions. The first is that the economic process can continue to produce greater resources to be shared, in whatever proportions, between capital, labour and welfare state provision. The second is that Social

Democracy can continue to believe that its redistributive goals are being achieved.

Although Marxists would tend to emphasise the first of these preconditions as the one which will cease to be operative and, thereby, undermine the Social Democratic strategy, it seems to me that, since the late 1960s, the Social Democrats have increasingly come to doubt the capacity of a combination of economic growth and social welfare reform as a sovereign remedy to cure the ills of capitalism. Beginning with New Left criticisms of inadequacies in the existing welfare system, there has been a 'rediscovery of poverty' (Hancock, 1972, p. 82). It was this which was the impetus for the many low incomes studies that have taken place in the Scandinavian countries in the last decade. Their findings, some of which I have reported, have been sufficient to shake any complacency felt by Social Democrats about the extent of their egalitarian achievement. This has led to a search for new strategies to attack all forms of social inequality. Partly, this has involved a reintensification of previous efforts. The knowledge provided by studies of income distribution has made it possible to direct the welfare effort more consciously to sub-groups for the population most at risk from a low incomes point of view. For instance, studies have tended to emphasise the difficulties of the disabled or partially disabled in finding full-time employment, and special efforts have been made to devote industrial training resources to these individuals, and where necessary to create sheltered employment. This has now become an important function of the Labour Market authorities in their pursuit of an 'active' labour market policy. Thus welfare objectives have been added to the goals of industrial efficiency and full employment that such policies are already designed to serve. Such a change in orientation is explicit in the Swedish Labour Market Board's view that its functions have ceased to be merely the provision of jobs for those without them, but are 'within the framework of the need for labour power in society, to give each who can and wants to work the effective support to realize his free choice of employment' (cited by Heclo, 1974, p. 139).

Where low income groups include much more substantial proportions of the population, the problems are commensurately more difficult to resolve. As I mentioned earlier, it is intended that Norwegian agricultural incomes should reach the levels averaged by industrial workers within five years, but this involves an enormous transfer of the resource balance which can almost certainly only be contemplated because of Norway's expected oil revenues. However, under less fortunate economic circumstances, major redistributions can only be affected by imposing a politically intolerable tax burden on the middle strata or by challenging the prerogatives of the privileged. It has been in the latter direction that Social Democratic strategy has been tentatively shifting in recent years.

The method chosen has involved a focus on the third dimension of Scandinavian welfare objectives: the decrease in the cumulative impact of inequalities in the different components of the level-of-living. If, as T. H. Marshall argues, the expansion of citizenship rights in the last two centuries has involved a progression from civic to political to social rights, then one may characterise recent Social Democratic policy as the early stages of an attempt to confer industrial and economic rights of citizenship. The logic of the attempt is underlined by the findings of many of the low incomes studies that poverty is associated with a wide variety of other types of deprivation including poor health, low educational level, an undesirable work *milieu,* inability to participate in decisions affecting one's own life-chances and absence of political resources.[18] The emerging Social Democratic strategy stance sees the progressive removal of deprivation of these kinds as an inherent goal of equality policy, but it focuses on the industrial and economic aspects of deprivation in the belief that these are not merely consequences but also, to some extent, causes, of the inegalitarian distribution of incomes in society.

An emphasis on industrial rights of citizenship — *industrial democracy* — is seen as the appropriate political response to the most flagrant locus of inequality in contemporary society. The Alva Myrdal Report to the Swedish Social Democratic Party on the problems associated with creating an egalitarian society puts it thus:

> In the workplace society's inequalities show up more clearly than anywhere else. The differences in influence are there — a small group of owners formally commands all the power and the right to make decisions about the means of subsistence of the vastly greater number of employees. In the workplace we find the hierarchy which is being broken down in other parts of society — individuals are arranged in a structure of obedience relationships. By means of differential arrangements of benefits — wages, social benefits, different travelling and expenses allowances, varying access to information, various grades of individual freedom and responsibility, etc. — gaps are created between categories of people, who as a result form subgroups instead of a large working community. . . . Without a policy determined to counteract these inequalities, the gaps will continue to grow and new ones will develop (Myrdal, 1971, p. 107).

Such policies have constituted much of the legislative output of the Scandinavian polities in the last few years, and have also dominated the negotiations between trade unions and employers. Although the new policy emphasis has varied somewhat from country to country, a number of general themes emerge in all of them. Worker or trade union representatives are now on the boards of all the larger companies. Worker representation is in no case seen as giving employees a decisive role in the running of the company, but is rather intended to provide an institutionalised setting in which employee opinion can be voiced and, probably more crucial, in which employees can gain access to company plans for future operation. Various rules have been elaborated to give employees longer periods of notice of dismissal, provide special protection for older workers (in Norway a worker who is over sixty and has been with an enterprise for ten years gets a minimum of six months notice), and ensure that employers have just grounds for giving notice of dismissal. In respect of working conditions, the general rationale of legislation has been that the working environment should be 'fully defensible' as such. Not only have employers been required to obviate hazardous working conditions, but 'protection ombudsmen' are chosen from among the workers with the right to stop production where there appears to be any risk to the safety of employees. Finally, the employer's sole right to control his enterprise has been challenged. In 1973, the new Basic Agreement between the Danish Employers' Confederation (DA) and LO modified the long-standing 'right of the employer to direct and distribute the work' so that it must now be exercised 'in accordance with the content of the collective agreements and in cooperation with the employees and their shop stewards as provided by current agreements between LO and DA' (Kuhlmann, 1974, pp.43-4). Legislation which had a similar content, and specifically giving the trade unions the right to reach collective agreements on non-wage issues, was the last major policy enactment of the Swedish Social Democrats before coming to the end of their long tenure in office.

Industrial democracy can be seen as a major contribution to welfare in the sense of decreasing the inequalities in working conditions and of giving employees a greater access to decision-making processes which affect their livelihoods. It is not, however, clear whether, even in the long-run, such measures will be conducive to altering the reward structure of capitalism. It is in a direct effort to make changes in the distribution of economic rewards that policies for *economic democracy* have been recently proposed. Such proposals involve schemes to share the wealth and power accruing to the ownership of capital. Although they cannot be regarded as nationalisation in the conventional sense of state ownership and dispossession of existing owners, they involve a gradual and, eventually, substantial dispersion of the rights stemming from the ownership and control of industrial capital. Two variants of the economic democracy proposals exist: the Danish and the Swedish. The

Danish scheme is basically a form of profit-sharing, whereby employers contribute a stipulated sum to a wage earners' fund which gives equal shares to all employees. Shares can be withdrawn after seven years, but there are tax incentives for leaving shares in the fund for a longer period. The fund would be administered by a board consisting primarily of members elected by wage earner organisations and from the Ministry of Labour, and its resources would be invested in industry. A scheme of this kind is official Danish Social Democratic Party and LO policy, and its objectives are to share the rewards from capital ownership more equally and, to the degree that the fund progressively becomes a major share-holder in companies, to use its enhanced board representation to secure a more extensive codetermination in industry. The Swedish proposal is not Social Democratic policy, but is the accepted view of the LO. It involves an 'equalisation fund' which would be financed by an 'annual transfer of share capital equivalent to approximately 20 per cent of pre-tax profits earned by firms employing a specified number of workers' (see Hancock, 1977, p. 21). The fundamental differences from the Danish scheme are that it would not be a profit-sharing scheme and that the fund would be more centrally controlled by the trade unions. Within twenty to thirty years, the trade unions would have a controlling interest in much of Sweden's industry, and redistributive policy would be effected not by a share in capital but by the direct manipulation of the wage structure by the controlling agency of the fund. It should be noted that this so-called 'Meidner Plan', whilst only being considered by the Social Democrats at the time of the 1976 election, was thought by many commentators to have contributed to the Party's electoral defeat.

It would be wrong to conclude from this very brief discussion of industrial and economic democracy policies that the whole emphasis of the traditional Social Democratic strategy has changed. What has emerged from the debate on equality in Scandinavia in the last decade is that the existing reformist strategy combining social welfare and economic growth is not by itself sufficient to bring about an egalitarian society. At a minimum, the traditional strategy must be supplemented by an attempt to begin to reshape the fundamental industrial and economic relationships that determine a large part of social inequality. However, there is no evidence that the Scandinavian Social Democratic parties have any intention to depart from their long-cherished ideals of social harmony and democracy. The question for the future is whether the conditions which permitted a peaceful development towards a society with a high level of welfare state provision will be as propitious for a gradual but basic change in the economic system of capitalism.

2.5 Capitalism and the Social Democratic image of society

This chapter set out to investigate whether Social Democratic political ascendancy in Scandinavia had produced results beneficial to the working class. Despite the considerable inequalities which remain in the distribution of incomes in Scandinavia, a substantial element of the industrial working class make up a part of the broad middle stratum of society. Indeed, as I noted previously, there are real dangers that this element may become the potential clientele of parties opposing further welfare or egalitarian reform as has happened to some extent in Denmark. The emergence of such a political orientation cannot be comforting to the Social Democrats, but in a sense it is a testimony to their success. That success is also apparent in international perspective. The Scandinavian countries, together with the Netherlands, manifest a considerably higher level of welfare state provision than other advanced nations. To the extent that it was primarily the working class which, in the past, suffered most greatly from inequalities in status in respect of health provision, access to education and family welfare, this is an achievement which socialists cannot gainsay, despite the fact that it is an achievement compatible with ideologies other than socialism. Finally, the 'rediscovery of poverty' is not an exclusively Scandinavian phenomenon, but it is arguable that the Scandinavian Social Democrats have engaged in a more fundamental reappraisal of their strategy than have other Western European democratic socialist parties. That reappraisal has led to a renewed concern with the transformation of the industrial and economic structure of capitalism.

Having said this much in acknowledgement of the achievements of Scandinavian Social Democracy, it is interesting to return briefly to Parkin's 'agnostic approach'. It must be conceded at once that his most important criticism of Social Democracy – its failure to equalise the distribution of incomes – is born out by the Scandinavian studies of income distribution discussed previously. The combined impact of taxation and transfer payments do have a real impact in diminishing the gulf separating the rich and the poor, but there remain vast differences in the economic rewards accruing to individuals via the market mechanism. However, Parkin's view that 'West European countries dominated by Right and Centre governments in the post-war period do not necessarily allocate a smaller share of their national resources to welfare than do countries which have governments of the Left' (Parkin, 1971, p. 126) is refuted by the comparative data presented earlier in this chapter. It was partly on the basis of the supposed failure of democratic socialist governments to achieve higher levels of welfare than administrations of a more right-wing complexion that Parkin argues that democratic socialist parties have become effectively deradicalised. He does not regard an emphasis on welfare state provision as a *strategy option* amenable to change under new conditions, but as part of 'a major transformation in the moral and political outlook of the socialist movement' (Parkin, 1971, p. 127). This seems more dubious in light of the Scandinavian experience. The only three democratic socialist parties which have succeeded in establishing their political dominance can reasonably claim that their emphasis on welfare reform and economic growth has paid real dividends for the working class. To that extent their policy stance can be seen as a defensible socialist strategy option. Naturally, over several decades, what the Scandinavian Social Democrats originally saw as a profitable option became more and more a part of the collective experience and outlook of the respective labour movements, but the crucial point is that under the pressure of the 'rediscovery of poverty' they have begun to rediscover their radicalism and to modify their strategy in the direction of a more fundamental transformation of the capitalist system.

It should be noted that the achievements of the Scandinavian Social Democrats in the welfare field do not necessarily refute the contention that extensive welfare state provision is compatible with efficient capitalist production. Indeed, given the rather high economic growth rates experienced by Norway and Sweden in the postwar period, it might be argued that welfare reforms were positively conducive to industrial efficiency. Even where labour takes a somewhat larger share of the national income, and transfer payments have a net redistributive effect, high industrial productivity can still make entrepreneurship a remunerative vocation. This is, at least, the conclusion which seems to emerge from Assar Lindbeck's summing-up of the impact of redistributional efforts on the functioning of the Swedish industrial system.

> I think that the general lesson from the Swedish experiences, at least so far, is that *income redistribution can go quite far without serious losses in terms of economic efficiency and freedom for most individuals,* and in fact with considerable widening of the freedom of choice for previously underprivileged groups in society. For instance, a rather slow but continuous fall in the profit share, to some 10-15 percent of national income, seems to have been reconcilable with a fairly dynamic economy. And, in particular, a rather substantial narrowing of the differentials in *disposable incomes,* and per capita consumption by households by way of tax-transfer systems, have been possible without apparent drastic losses in incentives for work and efficient allocation of labor (Lindbeck, 1975, pp. 362-3).

The fact that social welfare is compatible with efficient capitalist enterprise is frequently taken by left-wing commentators to imply that welfare cannot be considered as an integral part of the socialist achievement. As I have mentioned before, this seems absurd to the degree that welfare is considered a socialist objective and it can be shown that some societies — ones in which democratic socialist parties are dominant — have a greater degree of welfare than others. The left-wing contention involves an *a priori* assumption that different classes cannot have any interests in common. Whether classes can co-operate in achieving certain objectives seems to me to be a question which must ultimately be resolved as much by empirical as by theoretical analysis. At some periods, and given certain structural and historical preconditions, such co-operation may be possible, whilst other times and circumstances may be more conducive to class antagonism.

The structural and historical circumstances favouring Scandinavian Social Democratic political dominance and a reformist strategy are the subject of the next chapter, but before turning to the origins of the Social Democratic achievement, I wish to make a few concluding remarks about the future prospects of welfare and equality in the Scandinavian countries.

Again Parkin's views provide a convenient focus for discussion. He asserts that the 'eventual acceptance by the dominant political class' of educational reforms and welfare measures 'rests on quite different grounds' from the egalitarian reasons that such proposals are advanced by democratic socialists (Parkin, 1971, p.127). They are accepted because they contribute to industrial efficiency, lessen radical discontent and do not have the dramatic redistributive impact of direct attacks on property rights. This may well be a fairly accurate characterisation of the situation in the vast majority of advanced nations, but it has two serious deficiencies as a description of Scandinavian political reality.[19]

The first is the implicit equation between the capitalist class and the 'dominant political class'. After four or more decades that seems just a little too sweeping a judgment. Scase, of whom I was otherwise rather critical, makes the point excellently in the context of a comparison between Britain and Sweden.

> Although Sweden and Britain are both capitalist countries it is not to be assumed that they have exactly comparable power structures. In Sweden, the development of an influential working-class movement has increased the representation of industrial manual workers in the governmental decision-making process and thus restricted the emergence of a national power structure in which political and economic interests are closely interrelated in pursuing the interests of private capital. In other words, the state is less dominated by the

interests of the privately owned economy than it is in Britain (Scase, 1977, p. 163).

The representation of the industrial working class in the state apparatus is not merely a question of a strong parliamentary presence. Social Democrats and their sympathisers are integrated into the institutional machinery at all levels. They constitute a sizable proportion of the higher state bureaucracy, the provincial administrations, the judiciary and, indeed, every major political instrumentality in Scandinavia. Exactly the same is true at the local and intermediate levels. Within the schools, the decisive voice in administration and curriculum development is as likely to be Social Democratic as bourgeois. In the factories, as has been mentioned, recent legislation has given the decisive responsibility in regard to safety to the workers rather than the employer. This permeation of the state and, even to some degree, the industrial structure, by the representatives of the organised working class makes it inconceivable that temporary election losses by the Social Democrats will have any impact on either the existing level of welfare state provision or the impetus for this type of reform.

Moreover, the longstanding political dominance of the Scandinavian Social Democrats has another extremely significant implication. It has always been a fundamental tenet of socialist doctrine that the capitalist class uses its control of the state apparatus not only to underwrite its economic ascendancy, but also to guarantee its ideological hegemony. The 'image of society' purveyed through the agencies of political socialisation is seen as one which reinforces the capitalist values of the dominant class and preaches the virtues of political passivity to the masses.[20] But in Scandinavia the dominant political class is not capitalist in orientation. Some of the agencies of political socialisation — for instance, a substantial portion of the press — remain in private hands. However, many others do not. Radio and television are administered by a 'politically neutral' agency, which like virtually every 'politically neutral' body in Scandinavia attains that status in virtue of its reflection of the prevailing political balance: in other words, Social Democratic dominance. The schools and all the other state-sponsored agencies through which the citizen learns the socially appropriate codes of conduct are 'politically neutral' in just the same sense. As a consequence, it can be argued that the dominant 'image of society' may aptly be described as basically Social Democratic in character.

To give a single example of the difference this can make, one can contrast the attitudes to social security provision in Britain and Sweden. In Britain, one of the greatest problems faced by those who administer the various welfare services for the needy is that those who have a legal claim to benefits frequently do not come forward to take advantage of them. This phenomenon is generally attributed to a mixture of lack of information and unwillingness to apply for 'charity'. It is difficult to imagine more eloquent testimony to the effectiveness of a political socialisation process which purveys capitalist values. In Sweden, in contrast, part of the curriculum taught in all comprehensive schools involves social studies courses which teach teenagers about the range of benefits to which the citizen is *entitled*. This single example, which could be multiplied for every area in which there is an implicit or explicit learn-process relating to the welfare and equality of citizens, suggests to me that the creation of a Social Democratic image of society may in itself be a socialist achievement of some magnitude.

The implications of the existence of a Social Democratic image of society can be regarded as the more significant as a consequence of the second deficiency in Parkin's portrayal of non-socialist attitudes to welfare and egalitarian reform. Parkin seems to assume that bourgeois governments constitute a single undifferentiated instrumentality of the dominant economic class. *That assumption only holds where there is a strong party of the Right.* The previous discussion in this chapter demonstrated that such a party acted as a major impediment to a high level of welfare state reform. The explanation of that finding may be located in the impact of divergent images of society. A strong party of the Right is the 'political arm of the capitalist movement' and it functions as much to foster a capitalist image of society as it does to block redistribution of economic rewards. Where, as in the Netherlands and Scandinavia, the capitalist class is unable to dominate the political process and state apparatus, it is possible that welfare and egalitarian values will come to occupy an important place in the dominant image of society. Indeed, on the basis of a Marxist analysis, there is no reason to believe that they will not. After all, the proletariat, in Marx's sense of those whose only marketable commodity is their labour power, constitute the vast majority of the population in all advanced societies. It is not obvious that the clientele of the parties of the Centre are intrinsically opposed to egalitarian reform, and it is still less so when the agencies of political socialisation are partially controlled by those who propagate egalitarian values.

It would be misleading to suggest that the Scandinavian bourgeois parties have political aims identical to those of the Social Democrats. The various parties' different clienteles — workers, small and larger farmers, routine and upper white-collar employees, and entrepreneurs — have different interests and political demands. As was demonstrated previously, the mechanisms of corporate pluralism exist precisely to permit accommodations between different social groupings. However, the balance of interests is never static. As compromise is reached on one issue and the parties move on to new areas of disagreement, they learn to live with, then to accept, and ultimately to embrace what was originally a compromise about which they had grave reservations. Such compromises have been by no means in one direction. The Social Democrats made the first concession the adoption of a reformist stance but, in four decades of Social Democratic political dominance, the values which have been consolidated as accepted elements in the prevailing image of society have moved progressively towards welfare and egalitarianism.

This, in a sense (but see note 19), explains some of the paradoxes of the contemporary Scandinavian political scene: the introduction by Norwegian bourgeois parties of fully comprehensive education, the massive welfare spending of the Danish bourgeois government in the late 1960s, and the assistance given the Swedish Social Democrats by the Liberals and Centre Party in pushing through industrial democracy legislation in a parliament, which between 1973 and 1976 was equally divided between socialist and non-socialist forces. The British reader who remains unconvinced of the singularity of Scandinavian politics might like to speculate on the probabilities of a moderate Conservative administration in Britain, such as that led by Edward Heath, taking any of these actions – much less one led by Margaret Thatcher.

The survey studies of elite attitudes in Scandinavia confirm a picture of bourgeois parties which oppose Social Democracy on many issues – taxation, decentralisation, stimulation of private enterprise – but share important egalitarian and welfare goals. Hancock, in a series of interviews with elite leaders of the Social Democratic Party, bourgeois parties, mass media, civil service, trade unions and business in Sweden, found a number of divergencies, which could clearly be explained in terms of a traditional Left-Right continuum. However, the major feature of expressed elite preference for domestic policy change in the 1970s was considerable agreement on the need for increased influence for employees, including industrial democracy and an improved workplace milieu, as well as improved planning of total resources (Hancock, 1976, p. 177). Similarly, research in Norway in the late 1960s again finds that there are certain differences between socialist and non-socialist elites, but notes that:

> The significant point, however, is that two-fifths of ostensibly non-socialist business and political leaders, and a majority of the civil service elite showed little reluctance to deny a central tenet in the liberal indictment of the welfare state, while only small minorities of these same non-socialist groups would flatly endorse that tenet (Higley et al., 1976, p. 288).

It is quite probable that the authors of neither of these studies would concede that the emergent consensus was indicative of a distinctive Social Democratic image of society, since both studies view attitude change as a concomitant of 'post-industrial' development. However, the former conclusion might seem more appropriate if one contrasts the attitudes of Scandinavian non-socialist elites with a British Conservative Party which preaches the old virtues of financial orthodoxy and the new orthodoxy of the virtues of 'monetarism', and a German Christian Democratic Party which by its recent election slogan, 'Freedom or Socialism', showed that it had not yet fully come to terms with Social Democracy's role in the political system.

The future prospects of Scandinavian Social Democracy are made more difficult to predict by the new issues and party alignments that have emerged in recent years. Even though the established bourgeois parties share in the welfare consensus, the taxation issue constitutes a threat to a redistribution policy which has financed welfare transfers as much from the middle strata as from the economically privileged. Quite apart from this issue, however, the Social Democrats are progressively reshaping their strategy in ways which will procure greater industrial and economic democracy. The latter, in particular, involves a considerable departure from the existing consensus, and is bound to be fiercely resisted by the employers and the Conservative parties. This does not necessarily mean that a gradual transformation of the economic structure of capitalism will not take place under democratic auspices in Scandinavia over the next few decades. Whether it does will depend on the capacity of the Social Democrats to arrive at compromises with the more progressive elements of the political Centre which will mobilise the prevailing image of society still further in an egalitarian direction. Past Social Democratic achievement is perhaps some testimony that success in this effort is more likely in Scandinavia than it might be elsewhere.

Part two:

Origins

Parties are the central intermediate and intermediary structure between society and government. Furthermore, insofar as they are a system, parties interact and such interactions can be viewed as mechanical propensities, as structures of rewards and opportunities that go a long way toward explaining the different performances of different types of party politics. Finally, I assume politics to be an independent variable, thus implying that parties and party systems mold (beyond the point at which they reflect) the political society. That is, before treating politics as a dependent variable it behooves the political scientist to explore how much mileage is afforded by its autonomy.

(Giovanni Sartori, 1976, pp. ix-x)

There is probably not in the history of mankind another instance of a free constitution, not erected amidst ruins and revolution, not cemented with blood, but taken from the closet of the philosopher and quietly reared and set to work, and found to be suitable without alteration to all the ends of good government. The reason for this apparent singularity is that all the essential parts of liberty were already in the country. The property was in the hands of the whole body of the people. The ancient laws and institutions affecting property were in full operation, and were conceived and administered in the very spirit of liberty. . . . There was nothing in the condition of the people, the state of property, the civil or religious establishments, which did not fit in with a free constitution in which legislative power was vested in the people. These had all emanated from the people in ancient times; and, there being no hereditary privilege, no power vested in any class of the community, had been handed down unbroken through the ages.

(Samuel Laing, *Journal of a Residence in Norway during the Years 1834, 1835 and 1836*)

3

Paradoxes of Scandinavian political development

Scandinavian politics since the 1930s has been characterised by an unique combination of features: a high level of relative dominance of democratic socialist parties and a marked achievement in the field of welfare state provision. To many commentators the link between these phenomena borders on the obvious. It is because Scandinavian Social Democracy has pursued the path of gradual parliamentary reform that it has reaped the fruits of the consistent electoral victory required to implement its welfare goals. At times this strategy has meant moving forward 'at the pace of a tortoise'. However, in a longer perspective, it has guaranteed slow but ineluctable progress towards a more humane and egalitarian society. Already the industrial working class are firmly entrenched within the state apparatus and, assuming only that Social Democracy can, as it has in the past, arrive at compromises with other social groups, there is no inherent reason why the Social Democratic image of society should not eventually be broadened further to include the basic industrial and economic rights of citizenship. In such a view, socialism and social harmony may not be as irreconcilable as some on both Left and Right have tried to suggest.

As will have been self-evident from the preceding analysis, I have great sympathy for the *values* implicit in this conception of the role of democratic socialism. If an egalitarian society can only be achieved at the cost of the abdication of political liberty and democratic rights then the calculus of political choice must become an intolerable burden. It would be more felicitous to believe, with the philosophers of the eighteenth century, in the inevitable victory of reason, or with Marx, that nothing of human value is lost in the dialectical progress toward a higher stage of social development. However, the evidence of political life in the twentieth century provides little cause for such optimism. Those who have pursued social and economic equality by violence have created societies in which political freedom and equality of citizenship have no reality and in which the level of social equality is itself not beyond reproach. True, they, like the Scandinavian Social Democrats, can point to achievements compared with the past; but it is a bloody and tyrannical past. Western societies have not pursued the path of violence — except perhaps in oppressing non-Western societies — but then neither have they made appreciable progress in the creation of a humane and egalitarian society. It might even be better for humanity if economic development were the sufficient cause of enhanced welfare since, that being so, the advanced nations of the West might well manifest a greater level of welfare than is common today.

Only in Scandinavia have democratic socialist parties made any real impact on the basic political mechanism by which the economically dominant class secures its hegemony. In Denmark, Norway and Sweden:

> Power and privilege have largely been separated: those who enjoy the greatest measure of political power no longer enjoy the greatest measure of economic privilege, and those who enjoy the greatest measure of economic privilege tend to the weak politically (Lenski, 1966, p. 326).

Clearly, the gap between the existing level of achievement and the socialist goal of an egalitarian society is enormous ('But we have *not* gone very far if you want your dream of a classless society to come true. In that case, most of the work remains to be done!'), but at least the state is no longer the instrumentality of economic oppression. *Perhaps* it will be possible to build on the achievement of the past to create the basis for a truly humane society.

However, neither sympathy for the values of democratic socialism nor a demonstration that reformist strategy has been successful in Scandinavia are sufficient conditions of a belief that such a strategy must be as effective elsewhere. It seems to me that if Marxist analysis must often be condemned for undue economic determinism, then reformist views tend to suffer no less from a rather naive political voluntarism. To believe that an emulation of Scandinavian Social Democratic success is merely a question of adopting an appealing electoral posture — avoid nationalisation like the plague and pile on the welfare — involves one of two alternative assumptions: either that all advanced nations have identical political structures or that historical experience has no impact on contemporary political action. The very fact of four decades of Social Democratic political dominance in Scandinavia refutes the first and the undistinguished record of reformist effort outside Scandinavia may go some way toward casting doubt on the second.

The remaining sections of this book will examine the structural and historical context in which Scocial Democratic dominance and a successful reformist policy have emerged in Scandinavia. The focus will be particularly on the basis of party support, the interactions of parties and organised groups, the cleavage structure which has shaped party divisions and the historical conditions that have hindered the development of a Bourgeois image of society.[1] In other words, I will attempt to explain the singularity of contemporary politics in Scandinavia in terms of a syndrome of structural and historical circumstances which only they have in common (Mill, 1967, p. 255). At the conclusion of my enquiry, I do not intend to discuss the relevance of the Scandinavian experience for democratic socialist parties elsewhere in Europe. By that time, it should be evident that the Scandinavian experience has very little relevance outside Scandinavia.

3.1 Class and party in Scandinavia

The strength of a political party is a function of its own electoral position and the nature of the opposition it faces from other parties. At a formal level, chapter 1 demonstrated that Social Democratic ascendancy was a consequence of the fact that, alone of European democratic socialist parties, those of Scandinavia consistently attracted approximately 40 per cent of electoral support and maintained a high level of relative dominance over the next largest party in the system. In this section these findings will be examined in somewhat greater detail.

The immediate paradox which emerges is that the paragons of reformist virtue are in one sense the most distinctively working-class parties in Europe. This is not meant to imply that the Scandinavian Social Democrats do not attract votes from other occupational groups, but rather that they attract a greater percentage of working-class votes than do other European democratic socialist parties. It is extremely difficult to present comparable data on the socialist share of the working-class vote because of the wide divergencies in occupational categorisations. However, the contrasts which are revealed by the data which are available are sufficiently dramatic to warrant explanation in terms other than mere differences in statistical definition. Table 3.1 presents data on the share of the working-class vote attracted by democratic socialist parties in eight European countries. The figures for all countries except Denmark are derived from the surveys of electoral behaviour reported by the authors who contributed to the comparative handbook on *Electoral Behaviour* edited by Richard Rose. The authorship of each study, the date of the survey material and the page reference in Rose are indicated in the text of Table 3.1.

The development of integrated and united labour movements in Scandinavia was described in some detail in chapter 1, and it can now be seen that labour movement solidarity is a reflection of a high level of

Table 3.1 The share of the working-class vote attracted by democratic socialist parties in eight European countries

Country/Date	Party	Working-class vote %	Authorship of study and page reference
Belgium (1968)	Socialist Party	45	Keith Hill (p. 83)
Denmark (1968)	Social Democrats	62	Torben Worre*
Germany (1967)	Social Democrats	49	Derek Urwin (p. 147)
Finland (1966)	Social Democrats	42	Pertti Pesonen (p. 294)
Netherlands (1968)	Labour Party	37	Arend Lijphart (p. 243)†
Norway (1965)	Labour Party	68	Valen and Rokkan (p. 334)
Sweden (1968)	Social Democrats	75	Bo Särlvik (p. 401)
United Kingdom (1970)	Labour Party	51	Richard Rose (p. 502)

Sources: For all countries other than Denmark, Rose, 1974; for Denmark, Worre, 1977, p. 14.

*Worre's figures show a major decline in the Social Democrats' share of the working-class vote for 1973 and 1975. This is, of course, one of the causes of the Social Democratic election defeats in those years (see Table 1.4).

†Lijphart does not present a worker category. The figure is for socio-economic category C. For those who think it should be combined with the data for category D, the relevant percentage is 38.

working-class support for the Social Democratic parties. It is sometimes assumed that working-class support for a party of the left is in some sense a 'natural' phenomenon of politics in the contemporary era, but, as Table 3.1 demonstrates, it is obviously rather more natural in Scandinavia than elsewhere. Comparisons with the situation of the other democratic socialist parties represented in the table show that the major forces dissipating working-class unity are largely absent in Scandinavia.

There are no substantial minorities based on religion, language or ethnic origin in Scandinavia, which in many European countries have formed the basis of political parties with a cross-class appeal, and have offered an alternative focus of loyalty to sections of the working-class vote. The cross-class nature of religious parties in the Netherlands has already been noted in the context of that country's high level of welfare state provision, and may well be a partial explanation of the 'strength of the collective push for equality' in the Netherlands that is is the only country in Europe in which religious parties have consistently gained higher percentage of the working-class vote than the democratic socialists.[2] The surveys cited in Table 3.1 also show that religious parties in Belgium and Germany obtain in excess of 30 per cent of the working-class vote. In Belgium, the growing salience of the linguistic division has led to a decline in the parliamentary strength of all the traditional parties, including the Socialist Party (Heisler, 1974, p. 206). Where a party system reflects strong cultural fragmentation it is necessarily an impediment to democratic socialist political dominance. It is true that both Austria and Germany are countries in which cross-cutting religious influences have not prevented democratic socialist governments from assuming office, but that this has only occurred within the last decade is testimony enough to the divisive impact of religious parties on the working-class vote.

Nor is there evidence that the working class in the Scandinavian countries display any tendency towards deferential voting of the kind which is sometimes suggested as an explanation of working-class Conservatism in Britain. The deference thesis argues that the British Conservative Party is a beneficiary of a working-class allegiance based on the Party's alignment with dominant religious, economic and educational institutions (Parkin, 1967, pp. 278-90). Studies have suggested that, for whatever reasons, the British working class may be subject to severe cross-pressures.

> One might expect that in the working class electorate, Conservative voters would be more susceptible to conflicting pressures than Labour voters. But the evidence of this study tends in quite the opposite direction; it would seem that working class voters for Labour are typically more vulnerable to a sense of conflict or contradiction. Many Labour voters readily endorse the Labour party as an agent of their class interests but widely concede that the Conservatives are generally more competent and qualified in other respects, including the defence of the national interest; much less frequently, Conservatives concede such virtues to Labour (McKenzie and Silver, 1968, p. 247).

There has been some controversy about the specific validity of the deference explanation of working-class Conservatism, but none at all about the reality of the phenomenon.[3]

If there were any tendency for the working class in Scandinavia to give allegiance to the Conservative Party because of that Party's alignment with dominant values, one would expect it to have been more strongly manifested in the past before Social Democracy became entrenched in the power structure. However, a description of the relationship between class and party in Sweden some thirty years ago suggests that class solidarity was, if anything, stronger than today.

> With the increasingly static character of Swedish economic life, the concept of class solidarity has in some respects gained rather than lost in power over public opinion. In the eyes of many people, even if you manage to improve your position so as to alter your status, it is your duty to preserve your allegiance to the class in which you were born. . . . You owe allegiance to your class; it is therefore your sacred duty to belong to the organizations representing it, and to remain loyal to those organizations regardless of personal interests and opinions (Heckscher, 1948, p. 444).

However, if there has been any decline in class solidarity in Scandinavia in recent years, it seems to be more likely to be a consequence of non-working class strata voting for the Social Democrats than *vice versa*. The contemporary situation is depicted in Table 3.2 which presents data for party support according to occupational status in the three Scandinavian countries. Two significant features emerge from Table 3.2 in the context of the present discussion. First, if deference is simply seen as the propensity of working-class voters to identify with the party of the Right, it is virtually nonexistent in Scandinavia. Second, with the exception of the farmers, the non-working-class strata are more heterogenous in their party support than the working class. One might even like to think of a sort of deference in reverse measured by the extent of entrepreneurial and upper white-collar support for the Social Democrats. In Norway and Sweden, this phenomenon appears to be quite significant, although in Denmark it is somewhat less so. Uusitalo in his comments on these findings suggest that it is probably the owners of smaller enterprises and upper white-collar employees with working-class parents who support the Social Democrats (Uusitalo, 1975b, p. 23). Nevertheless, when the strong Social Democratic support amongst the lower white-collar strata is also taken into account, the contrast with Britain where 'Labour support within the working-class is not as strong as Conservative support within the middle-class' could hardly be greater (Rose, 1974, p.531). It should be added that the relatively strong support for the Social Democrats among virtually all non-farmer groups offers further empirical support for the argument that contemporary Scandinavian politics is characterised by the dominance of a Social Democratic image of society.

The only factor which has had any appreciable impact in dissipating

working-class unity and integration in Scandinavia has been the occasional rivalry of an alternative claimant to the working-class vote. The
early radicalism and schisms within the Norwegian Labour Party were

Table 3.2 Party support by occupational status in Denmark, Norway
and Sweden

Party support	Farmer	Entrepreneur	Upper white-collar	Lower white-collar	Skilled workers	Unskilled workers	All
Denmark: 1971							
Left	0	2	12	18	13	8	10
Social Democrats	2	19	9	31	61	81	34
Parties of Centre	79	27	43	21	16	12	35
Conservatives	19	52	36	31	8	-	20
Total	100	100	100	101	98	101	99
Norway:1969							
Left	1	0	9	5	7	8	6
Labour	9	42	21	40	72	72	44
Parties of Centre	84	27	28	31	14	20	31
Conservatives	6	31	42	25	6	-	19
Total	100	100	100	101	99	100	100
Sweden: 1970							
Left	2	5	1	2	3	7	3
Social Democrats	9	18	24	47	69	53	47
Parties of Centre	85	57	53	40	26	33	40
Conservatives	5	21	22	10	2	7	10
Total	101	101	100	99	100	100	100

Source: Uusitalo, 1975b, p. 21 and pp. 39-41. I have recalculated the figures for
the socialist parties to separate Left and Social Democrats.

noted in chapter 1. This had a significant effect in retarding the Party's
electoral progress in the 1920s compared with the other Scandinavian
Social Democratic parties. Nevertheless, as Ulf Torgersen has noted, it
is as important to emphasise the extremely rapid process of 'deradicali-
zation that brought the party membership in Comintern to the Cabinet
in the course of four years' (Torgersen, 1970, pp. 102-3). The emergence
of Socialist People's parties in Denmark and Norway was also discussed

in chapter 1. The data in Table 3.2 show that a significant proportion of the skilled workers in Denmark support parties to the Left of the Social Democrats. A similar impact is less apparent in the Norwegian data, but the date of the survey coincides precisely with the low ebb of the Socialist People's Party before the revitalisation of the EEC issue. Despite these instances of divisions within the ranks of the Scandinavian labour movements, they have remained relatively free of ideological schisms when viewed in comparative perspective.

The relevant contrast is with the Finnish experience. The Finnish Social Democratic Party receives only 42 per cent of the working-class vote, almost the lowest figure reported in Table 3.1. It is not, however, the only socialist party in Finland. The Finnish Peoples Democratic Union — basically, a Communist Party — in addition receives 34 per cent. Taking into account a small left-wing splinter group, the Social Democratic League, the working-class vote for the combined socialist parties is actually higher in Finland than in any other country included in Table 3.1. Finnish experience of ideological division within the labour movement has a dual significance as a comparative reference point for labour movement development in Scandinavia. First, it demonstrates the problems encountered by deeply divided socialist parties in translating votes into political office. The Social Democratic Party has normally been included in coalitions of the Centre during the postwar period, and the Finnish Peoples Democratic Union is one of the very few European Communist parties occasionally to participate in government. However, the crucial point is that, although the combined socialist parties have on two occasions won a majority of parliamentary seats (in 1958 and 1966), they have never been able to form distinctively leftish administrations, and have only been able to subdue their mutual antagonisms within the context of broad Left-Centre coalitions. Second, Finland has a special relevance to Scandinavia because until 1809 the country was an integral part of Sweden. The fact that it then became a Grand Duchy under Russian suzerainty and, thus, was actively implicated in the traumas of the Russian Revolution, is sufficient explanation for a deeply divided working class. However, to the extent that it can be argued that the present singularity of Scandinavian politics is a consequence of the shaping of party strengths and divisions by the context historical development, Finland should display a political configuration rather similar to that of the Scandinavian countries. This is, in fact, the case. The working class in Finland is undivided on religious and linguistic lines and shows the same disinclination to vote for Conservatives (Pesonen, 1974, p. 294). In addition, like Scandinavia, Finland's bourgeois parties are themselves divided, and the farmers have until recently provided strong support for a Centre Party which, in the context of

Finland's rather more agrarian economy and a divided working class, has played a more important political role than comparable parties in Scandinavia. Finally, prior to the Russian Revolution, Finland actually had the strongest Social Democratic party in Europe, which obtained 40 per cent of the vote as early as 1910. It would be wrong to make this point without noting that pre-First World War Finnish Social Democracy was both strengthened and radicalised by its position within the illiberal Tsarist state. Nevertheless, it may be a significant indication of the importance of Finland's Scandinavian heritage that the Social Democratic Party actually gained a parliamentary majority in 1916, whereas the chief victors in the elections to the Russian Constituent Assembly *after the 1917 Revolution* were the Socialist Revolutionaries, a primarily peasant party. Had it not been for the Russian Revolution, it seems probable that the subject of this book would have been the four dominant Social Democratic parties of Scandinavia and Finland.

The absence of significant religious, deferential and ideological divisions within the working class is the single most important cause of the Scandinavian Social Democratic parties' consistently high level of electoral support. It is not, however, the only cause. The Scandinavian social structures, as depicted by the percentage of the population falling into different occupational categories (see Table 2.9), are not sufficiently working class in composition to enable a purely working-class party to obtain anything approaching a parliamentary majority. To achieve office the Social Democratic parties must obtain non-working-class support. In the early stages of the parties' growth, when the countries had a more predominantly agrarian structure than today that support tended to come primarily from rural labourers, smallholders and fishermen. The contemporary situation is partially demonstrated by the data in Table 3.2 which show the percentage of different occupational strata supporting the Social Democrats. The raw data from which these percentages have been calculated can be recalculated to show the percentage of Social Democratic support which comes from non-working-class strata: in Denmark, 27 per cent, in Norway, 41 per cent and in Sweden, 38 per cent (Uusitalo, 1975b, pp. 39-41). In all three countries, the most sizeable non-working-class group supporting the Social Democrats is the lower white-collar stratum. In Norway and Sweden more of this group's votes go to the Social Democrats than to any other party, and the lesser degree of support in Denmark is not a consequence of non-socialist inclinations amongst this stratum, but rather a reflection of the curious ability of the Socialist People's Party to attract the lower white-collar vote. In recent years, there has been a tendency for the Scandinavian Social Democratic parties, and particularly the Swedish Party, to present themselves less as the exclusive agency of the industrial working class and more as the political voice of a 'wage-earners' front'. In light of the nature of the parties' strong lower white-collar support, that seems a hardly surprising development.

But, as has already been mentioned, the heterogeneity of Social Democratic support is noticeable even if the lower white-collar groups are considered as part of the proletarian stratum. Thus, as Henry Valen and Stein Rokkan point out, in Norway, the Scandinavian country with the highest level of non-working-class support for Social Democracy:

> The fact that a group of such heterogenous structure can be split-off on this one political criterion (the division between farmers and employers on one side and smallholders, fishermen, self-employed and higher-salaried employees) tells us something important about the cross-cutting character of the Labour Party. It not only attracts votes within the rural proletariat and among the smaller independents in the urban areas but has also established itself within the upper reaches of the municipal and national bureaucracy: *the party has been in or close to power for more than a generation and has been able to attract quite a few supporters in the higher echelons of the public sector* (Valen and Rokkan, 1974, p. 347. My italics).

A similar conclusion seems appropriate for Sweden where, according to Table 3.2, 18 per cent of the entrepreneurs and 24 per cent of the upper white-collar employees vote for the Social Democrats.[4] It is less appropriate in Denmark where the Socialist People's Party cuts into the upper as well as the lower white-collar vote. In general, it can be concluded that the electoral strength of the Scandinavian Social Democratic parties is not only a function of their strong working-class support, but also of the fact that they can make a cross-class appeal as a party of the whole nation. Thus, Scandinavian and British politics may be considered literally as mirror images of each other, for in the latter, it is the Conservative Party which bases its strength on its firm hold of the middle-class vote and makes its appeal as a party of the nation by attracting a substantial proportion of the working-class vote.

Electoral strength is a major aspect of the Scandinavian Social Democratic parties' political ascendancy; another is their large margin of relative advantage over other parties. Whereas the British, Austrian, and much more recently, the German democratic socialist parties have exhibited a level of electoral strength comparable to that of the Scandinavian Social Democrats, only the latter have consistently been the largest parties in their respective polities. The basic rationale for this difference is to be found in the nature of these countries' party systems. In Britain, Austria and Germany, democratic socialist parties are opposed by strong parties of the Right polling forty per cent or more of the vote. In contrast, the Scandinavian countries are characterised by party systems in which non-socialist opinion is fragmented into at least three separate parties. Bourgeois party disunity in Scandinavia is an expression both of divergent class interests and the heritage of past political conflicts.

A distinctive feature of the Scandinavian party systems compared with much of the rest of Western Europe has been the presence of parties representing the interests of the farming stratum. It is apparent from the data in Table 3.2 that farmers overwhelmingly support parties of the Centre. However, within this category, farmers have their own distinctive political instrumentality. In Denmark, it is the Liberal Party which receives 62 per cent of the farm vote; in Norway, the Centre Party (formerly, the Agrarian Party) obtains 64 per cent, and, in Sweden, the Centre Party (also formerly, the Agrarian Party) obtains 79 per cent (calculated from Uusitalo, 1975b, pp. 39–41). Denmark is the only one of the Scandinavian countries which manifests a marked economic differentiation in the agricultural sector, and there is a tendency for the richer farmers with a number of employees to support the Conservative Party. In Norway, the Centre Party has some competition for the farm vote from the Christian People's Party. Despite such differences, the farmers' parties of Scandinavia are quite clearly class parties in the same sense as the Social Democrats: they represent the interest of a distinct occupational group. The farmers' interests are similar to those of primary producers the world over: higher agricultural prices and cheaper industrial products. As such, farmers' interests are opposed to those of both capitalists and the industrial working class. In this context, it is significant that, with the exception of the more commercially orientated farmers in Denmark, the tendency for farmers to vote for either Conservatives or socialists is negligible. Moreover, there is another factor, noted in the previous chapter, which makes the gulf between the farmers' parties and the Conservatives difficult to bridge. If the farmers are ranged against both workers and capitalists on the primary versus secondary economy dimension, on the distribution of incomes dimension they have far more in common with the workers. Table 2.9 showed that in Norway and Sweden farmers have an incomes level comparable to unskilled workers, whilst, in Denmark, it is closer to that of skilled workers. Such data almost certainly exaggerate the low income status of farmers, since agricultural occupations generally provide a high level of non-taxable fringe benefits, but if the farming stratum was to be described as 'petit-bourgeois' it would have to be the prefix that was stressed.

It is significant that both the Swedish and Norwegian Social Democratic parties assumed power in the 1930s as a consequence of 'Crisis Agreements' with the Agrarians designed simultaneously to lower the level of unemployment and maintain the level of agricultural incomes. The situation in Denmark was somewhat different because the Social Democrats were already in coalition with the Radical-Liberals, a party which itself had substantial support from the poorest stratum in the farming community. However, even there, the settlement of the 1930s was largely based on the Liberals' willingness to support crisis measures in return for aid to agriculture. Today, the farmers' parties are ranged more firmly in the bourgeois camp, but, as was suggested in chapter 1, the Norwegian and Swedish Centre parties are amongst the most vociferous opponents of Social Democratic and Conservative policies which are seen as sacrificing the primary economy and the wider environment to the technocratic imperatives of industrial production. Needless to say, they are also supporters of redistribution to low income groups; not least, to those with low agricultural incomes.

The farmers' parties are, in one sense, more clearly class parties, at least in Denmark and Norway, than the Social Democrats, in so far as they draw little support from outside the agricultural *milieu*. This was also true of the Swedish Centre Party until about the mid-1950s. Since that time, the Party has succeeded in escaping its rural enclave and has encroached seriously on both the Liberal and Conservative support. In general, the divisions between the farmers' parties and the Liberal parties (Radical-Liberal in Denmark) are much less substantial than those which separate both from the Conservative parties. Both trace their origins to the Liberal movements, whose major achievement was the democratisation of the political systems in the late nineteenth and early twentieth centuries. To oversimplify not a little, the farmers' parties consisted of those who, having achieved democratic representation, felt the basic task was the representation of the interests of the primary economy, whilst the Liberals retained those social groups who felt that there remained an important role for a party of moderate social reform located somewhere in the political spectrum between the extremes of Social Democracy and Conservatism. Today, the Liberal parties in Sweden and Norway, and the Radical-Liberals in Denmark, are primarily urban middle-class parties. However, they retain a degree of radicalism, as has been demonstrated by the Danish Party's strongly neutralist stance in foreign affairs, and by the recent support afforded the Swedish Social Democrats by a Liberal Party which is as enthusiastic about many aspects of industrial democracy as the Social Democrats themselves.

The distance between farmers' parties and Liberals, the major parties of the Centre, and the Conservatives is partly one of class interest and partly one of historical tradition. The Conservatives draw on an almost exclusively urban clientele whose composition is heavily biased toward entrepreneurial and, particularly, upper white-collar groups. Within the Scandinavian political systems the Conservatives may be considered as the party of the Right in the sense that they most clearly express upper-class and employer interests. Although at an informal level, these parties maintain close links with the respective Employers' Confederations within each country. In historical terms, the Conservative parties are the direct descendents of the so-called 'Right' parties, which resisted, albeit with somewhat less vehemence than elsewhere in Europe, the assertion of the parliamentary principle and the extension of the suffrage. In so far as the parties of the Centre are all offshoots of the Liberal and 'Left' parties, whose great strength around the turn of the century was premised on their links with 'popular movements' dedicated to the democratisation of the polity, their self-identification is shaped as much by opposition to Conservatism as by divergence of interest from Social Democracy.[5]

The contrast with the relationship between the British Liberal and Conservative parties is instructive. The radical tradition of social liberalism is also part of the heritage of the British Liberal Party, but there are two crucial differences between that party and the Liberal/Liberal-Radical parties of Scandinavia. First, and most important, the British Liberal Party was not allowed to function as the distinctive instrumentality of popular pressure for democratic rights against the oligarchic prerogatives of a conservative ruling class. Disraeli by 'dishing the Whigs' not only laid the foundations for working-class Conservatism, but also undermined the basis for a lasting differentiation of the urban bourgeoisie in terms of divergent attitudes to established authority. Second, and largely as a consequence of this absence of differentiation, the British Liberal Party has declined far more rapidly than the offshoots of Scandinavian Liberalism. This difference cannot be explained in terms of varying electoral systems. The British Liberal Party is demonstrably the victim of the unfairness of the first-past-the-post system, but the point is that the adoption of proportional representation in Scandinavia was a direct consequence of the realisation that the bourgeois parties of the early decades of the twentieth century could not hope to find sufficient areas of agreement to form a united front against the growing might of Social Democracy. In Scandinavia, the parties of the Right came to see proportional representation as a 'conservative guarantee' hindering the rapid assumption of ministerial office by the representatives of the working class whilst, in Britain, a relatively undifferentiated urban bourgeoisie saw in the Conservative Party guarantee enough.

It might be argued that the changing social structure during the last half century has provided a stronger basis for a united bourgeois party given the necessary electoral engineering. Predictions of such a development have not been infrequent. Thus Valen and Katz suggested in 1964:

> The specific political set of institutions of parliamentarianism and of proportional representation will undoubtedly delay the movement towards a two-party system in Norway. Nonetheless, the larger forces in societal development are likely to prevail over time, and the long-run prediction is that the small parties in Norway will decline or coalesce to offer the voters the alternatives of centre-left and centre-right as in Britain and the United States (Valen and Katz, 1964, p. 41).

However, the recent pattern of party alignments in Scandinavia, as surveyed in chapter 1, suggest (if anything) that the prospects for bourgeois unity have diminished. In Norway itself, the Common Market issue served to reinforce the divisions between the parties of the Centre and the Conservatives. The historical separation between the Radical-Liberals and the other bourgeois parties in Denmark finally came to an end in 1968 but, in the new situation created by the intense fragmentation of the party system, the Social Democratic Party stays in office by obtaining the support of different bourgeois parties on each policy issue as it arises. In Sweden, there has been some degree of coalescence as measured by the growing strength of the Centre Party but, precisely because that growth has been based on the expansion of a farmers' party into the urban electorate, it has underlined the distinct identity of the parties of the Centre as contrasted with the Conservatives.

The persistent division between the Scandinavian bourgeois parties on grounds of class interest and historical tradition has given Social Democracy important advantages above and beyond those conferred by its electoral strength. Once the Social Democrats reached the 40 per cent level of electoral support, they were in a position where they needed only to detach or ensure the benevolent neutrality of one of the non-socialist parties in order to take office, whereas a bourgeois coalition required the agreement of three or more parties. Radical-Liberal support was a major contributory factor in Danish Social Democracy's fifteen-year tenure of office between 1953 and 1968. In Norway, there has been no postwar collaboration between the Labour and bourgeois parties, but before 1961 none was needed, since Labour had an absolute parliamentary majority. In Sweden, Social Democratic government was sustained for six years in the 1950s by a formal coalition with the Agrarian Party. Even when that coalition ended, and the parliamentary situation was extremely unfavourable to Social Democracy, the divisions between the bourgeois parties on the issue of the Social Democrats' proposed supplementary pension scheme made it possible for that legislation to be enacted. More recently, as already noted, the Swedish Liberals and Social Democrats reached an agreement on economic policy issues and industrial democracy, which tided a Social Democratic government over three years in which parliamentary forces were divided equally between socialists and non-socialists. Thus, the record of four decades of Scandinavian Social Democratic ascendancy demonstrates the decisive advantage for democratic socialism of a party system in which non-working-class electoral support is divided among a number of bourgeois parties. It should be added that this strategic advantage in coalition building is not appreciably diminished by the existence of small parties to the Left of the Social Democrats, since they rarely have any realistic option but to support the Social Democrats and attempt to exert what influence they can from the political sidelines.

In the context of the argument presented in chapter 2 that strong parties of the Right constitute an impediment to high levels of welfare state provision it should, finally, be noted that in Scandinavia the Conservatives form a minority even within the bourgeois camp. At no time since the 1930s have the Conservatives made up as much as half of a bourgeois government's parliamentary support. This point is of some significance, since it suggests that there will be strong pressures on the Conservatives to moderate their views rather than a tendency for the parties of the Centre to adopt a more right-wing stance. Immediately after the Second World War, both the Swedish and the Norwegian Conservative parties stressed the importance of a return to neo-liberal economic policies. In Sweden, this led to an election débâcle in which the Conservatives lost a substantial proportion of their voters to the Liberals. In Norway, a major political scandal ensued when it emerged that an organisation of conservative businessmen, propagandising for the principles of free enterprise, was directly financing the Conservative Party. Under heavy attack from the Labour press, which represented the affair as a capitalist conspiracy against the labour movement, and in fear of election losses on the Swedish scale, the Norwegian Conservatives hastily dissociated themselves from such a dubious ally (see Heidenheimer and Landon, 1968). Since the late 1940s, the Scandinavian Conservative parties have gradually been drawn into the welfare consensus. The last conspicuous attempt to resist a major welfare reform was the Swedish Conservative opposition to the Social Democratic superannuation proposals in the 1950s. The Conservatives suffered a reverse in the election of 1960, attributed by many commentators to the Party's strong defense of the principle of voluntary supplementary pensions, and in the wake of defeat announced that they now accepted the reform. In the following decade, the Conservatives reappraised their welfare stance and symbolised their revised orientation by a change of name to the Moderate Unity Party. In general, the conclusion that emerges from a survey of postwar Scandinavian Conservatism is that in these countries the parties of the Right can only fulfil their traditional role of the defence of privilege by a constant movement toward the consensus of the political Centre. The penalty for too strong a Conservative resistance is the loss of the electoral base which makes that role viable within the context of a democratic political system.

This section has demonstrated the close relationship between occupational class and party in Scandinavia. Whilst the Social Democrats are able to present themselves as parties of the whole nation in virtue of the votes they attract from all but the farming stratum, the fundamental basis of their strength is the support received from the vast majority of skilled and unskilled workers. The farmers' parties represent interests which are located on a somewhat different economic dimension from that which structures the conflicts of the occupational strata within the industrial economy, and this is an important guarantee of a distinctive presence in the political Centre. The Liberals and the Conservatives are divided by the historical legacy of past political conflicts, but also make a somewhat different appeal to the urban non-working-class vote, with the former being stronger among the lower white-collar employees and the latter gaining much of its support from upper white-collar employees and entrepreneurs. The significance of occupational status as an explanation of Scandinavian electoral behaviour has been noted by Richard Rose who, in a comparison of the effect of social structure on partisanship in fifteen advanced nations, shows that occupation has a considerably greater political impact in Scandinavia and Finland than elsewhere (Rose, 1974, p. 17). In Finland, the parties representing the working-class are divided but, in Scandinavia, Social Democratic parties representing the large majority of the working class have been politically dominant for nearly half a century. One of the paradoxes of Scandinavian political development is, thus, that the reformist Social Democratic parties of Scandinavia offer the only empirical confirmation of Marx's view that the politics of social class leads to the inevitable political victory of the working class.

3.2 The politics of virtuous circles

The strong influence of class in contemporary Scandinavian politics has not led to extensive class conflict, despite the seeming contradiction of a working-class party dominant in the political order and a capitalist class retaining control of 'the commanding heights of the economy'. Indeed, commentators have generally tended to emphasise compromise, stability and harmony as the characterising features of the Scandinavian societies. The paradox of the peaceful coexistence of a democratic socialist government and a capitalist economic order is resolved for the Left-wing by the argument that the Social Democrats have become effectively deradicalised and have failed to procure significant gains for the working class. Much of chapter 2 was devoted to a demonstration that this argument seriously misrepresented Scandinavian reality. The very existence of a paradox goes seemingly unnoticed by those right-wing socialists who advocate the emulation of the Scandinavian experience of socialism without social conflict *by de-emphasising democratic socialism's distinctive image as a party of the working class.* In this section, I shall attempt to show, in contradistinction to both shades of socialist opinion, that class politics is in large part a prior condition of political tranquillity and welfare reform — in Scandinavia, at least!

However, before turning to this discussion, I wish to examine briefly the most popular approach to the question of Scandinavian social harmony: the view that these countries have, in some sense, been conferred with the gift of grace. The theme that Scandinavia has been particularly fortunate has a number of variations. Sometimes the stress is on Scandinavia's cultural homogeneity, sometimes it is on an unbroken egalitarian tradition stretching far back into the mists of time, and sometimes it is on the countries' smallness. I do not wish to contend that any of these views is a false description of Scandinavian reality, although all but the last can easily be exaggerated. Moreover, I would argue that each contributes something to an understanding of the nature of Scandinavian political development. Indeed, I have already pointed to the absence of religious and linguistic divisions within the working class as a factor facilitating an integrated and unified labour movement. However, none of these views, nor all of them together, even begins to constitute a sufficient explanation of social harmony in Scandinavia.

Since the fallacy involved in all these 'explanations' is fundamentally similar, I shall take one as illustrative of all. This is the argument that 'small is beautiful'. Perry Anderson has put this case in a way which is explicit with regard to the implications for diminished class conflict.

Sweden — and this applies with extra force to Norway and probably to all the other Scandinavian countries — benefits from something quite different. This is as simple as the smallness of the population. The advantages of the 'local' community are up to a point transferred to the whole country. Collective hatreds depend partly on remoteness, on a kind of stylised and abstract image of the enemy. Sweden is a small enough country for the national link to be much more immediate than is the case here (i.e. in Britain). People are much more likely to be aware of members of an opposite group as individuals in their own right; this tempers the whole climate of class (Anderson, 1961, p. 12).

A similar argument has been put forward by Simon Kuznets to explain the high levels of economic growth of some small nations. He starts from the not infrequently advanced proposition that there are economic advantages in small size, but rejects this on the grounds that smallness makes it difficult to take advantage of the benefits of large-scale production, that the existence of any particular raw material asset necessarily has a transient effect, and that the ability to reap the benefits of the international division of labour is limited by the fact that many needed goods 'are closely interwoven with the country's distinctive culture and indigenous life [and] cannot be imported' (Kuznets, 1960, p. 27). He then goes on to suggest:

> [Given] the need for rapid and far-reaching social changes to take advantage of potentials of modern economic growth the small states are likely to have an easier task because of the closer ties among the members of their smaller populations; because of a possibly greater community of feeling among these smaller populations, due in part to a long background of common historical experience and in part to the lines of communication and connection among them that are closer than in a large country with its diversity of regions and multiplicity of local interests (Kuznets, 1960, p. 29).

That close community ties facilitate a lessening of class tensions and promote common effort toward economic goals is not necessarily incorrect, but the crucial point is that it is by no means always correct. This is implicit in the theory advanced by both authors that the closer are social ties, the less is the extent of social conflict. The analogy is with the family and other small group relationships which are generally regarded as the model of social harmony. But the analogy is not taken far enough for, whilst conflict within small groups is infrequent, when it does occur it tends to be extremely intense precisely because individuals are seen to be departing from established codes of social behaviour The Finnish civil war between 'Whites' and 'Reds' in the aftermath of the Russian Revolution, and the legacy of bitterness it contributed to Finish economic and political life for a generation, demonstrates clearly that small countries are not immune to the traumas of deep-rooted class conflict.

But it is not merely theoretical difficulties that make arguments from the various aspect of Scandinavia's good fortune so problematical. All fail to provide a sufficient explanation because they postulate invariant causes — cultural homogeneity, cultural heritage and small-ness — for a variable effect, Scandinavia's social harmony. The absence of class conflict, expressed variously in a low level of industrial disputes and inter-class compromises through the corporate pluralist mechanism, is a relatively new phenomenon. David Jenkins points to the basic nature of the fallacy in discussing the cultural explanations of the labour market peace for which Sweden is so justly famous.

> In groping for an explanation for this peculiarly peaceful atmosphere, some experts have opined that the lack of differences in race and religion between the two sides is the key. Perhaps, but if that is so, there is no clear reason why it should not have applied in the twenties, when Sweden's racial and religious make-up was even more homo-genous than it is now, *but when her work-stoppage record was considerably worse than in most other countries* (Jenkins, 1968, p. 134. My italics).

It is certainly arguable that the pre-industrial Scandinavian societies manifested strong social cohesion, and that the roots of many contem-porary institutional practices and attitudes can be traced back to this traditional heritage, but there was an intervening period, beginning with early industrialism and ending in the 1930s, in which political and industrial tension was very considerable. Thus, good fortune cannot be a sufficient explanation of social harmony, since Scandinavia re-mained fortunate when social harmony was lacking. At the most, such explanations point to background factors which help to reinforce social harmony when other circumstances are propitious.

Politics in Scandinavia before the 1930s was no less the politics of social class than it has been in subsequent decades, but the assumption of office by the Social Democrats marked a dramatic decline in class conflict. The strictly political manifestation of this phenomenon was discussed in chapter 1, where it was shown that the deep divide of the 1920s between the parties of economic orthodoxy and a Social Demo-cratic Party whose goal was to alleviate the situation of the unemployed, was resolved by the 'Crisis Agreements' of the 1930s. But the transfor-mation was, if anything, more dramatic in the case of industrial conflict. Prior to the 1930s all the Scandinavian countries were characterised by extremely high level of strike activity. Measured in terms of strike volume (i.e. strikers per 1,000 workers) and strike participation (i.e. strikers per 1,000 workers) the level of industrial conflict in the three decades 1900-30 was higher than in the majority of advanced nations.[6] Although Denmark was somewhat more peaceful than Norway and Sweden, the level of strike activity in the latter countries was com-parable to that of Britain, usually regarded as the epitomy of poor industrial relationships in the pre-1930 period.[7] Yet, in Denmark from the late 1920s, and in Sweden and Norway from the early 1930s, both strike volume and strike participation declined rapidly. Between 1945 and 1970, strike activity in Sweden and Norway was conspicuous by its absence, and the somewhat greater incidence in Denmark, reflecting the lower degree of labour movement cohesion in that country, can hardly be regarded as considerable in international perspective.

That there is a relationship between Social Democratic political dominance and a markedly reduced level of industrial tension can only be established by a comparison of strike activity in the advanced nations since the Second World War. The pioneering study in this field suggested that, in fact, there had been a general decline in strike activity in North West European nations in the postwar period, and not one restricted to countries with democratic socialist governments (Ross and Hartman, 1960). However, this finding has been challenged by a number of recent studies. Geoffrey Ingham has compared patterns of industrial conflict in Britain and Scandinavia, and argues that it is only in the latter that strike activity has 'withered' in all its forms (Ingham, 1974, p. 33). In a much wider study of twelve advanced nations, Douglas Hibbs suggests most significant findings.

> There is simply no evidence of a general decline or withering away of strike activity in industrial societies during the twentieth century. In six of the twelve countries — Canada, Finland, France, Italy, Japan and the United States — strike activity has either increased or fluctuated (often markedly) about a constant mean or equilibrium level. Industrial conflict has declined significantly in Belgium and the United Kingdom, *but has decreased to truly negligible levels only in Denmark, the Netherlands, Norway and Sweden.* Hence the withering away of the strike is a rather limited phenomenon confined largely to the smaller democracies of Northern Europe. Moreover, to the extent that strike data are relevant in making judgements about the state of class relations, the long-run trend results cast considerable doubt on macrosociological arguments about the integration of the working class into the social structure of advanced capitalist nations (Hibbs, Jr., 1976, pp. 15-16. My italics).

In other words, strike activity has only withered away and the working class become integrated into the structure of capitalist societies in the four countries identified in chapter 2 as those with the highest levels of welfare state provision. Hibbs, in an analysis which strikingly parallels and confirms my own, shows extremely strong 'correlations between growth of Social Democratic and Labor political power (percentage cabinet representation), the change in the locus of the distribution of national income (growth of the public sector share of the GNP), and change in strike volume . . . from the interwar to postwar period in ten countries' (Hibbs, 1976, p.32).[8] The data presented by Hibbs adds an historical dimension to the conclusions which were reached in chapter 2 by means of an exclusively cross-sectional comparison. The only slight disagreement that I would have with the analysis is that the method of presentation under-emphasises the political differences between the Netherlands and the Scandinavian countries. By choosing the interwar/postwar cutoff (necessarily imposed by any disputation of the Ross and Hartman findings) there is an inherent underestimation of the impact of the change to Social Democratic government in Scandinavia in the 1930s.

The close relationship between declining strike activity and high welfare state provision in Scandinavia and the Netherlands is most significant because, in the Scandinavian case, it offers clear evidence of the successful operation of one of those mechanisms on which Social Democratic strategy has been based. In chapter 1, it was argued that the solidarity of the two arms of the labour movement was a crucial precondition of that strategy. In the confidence that the Social Democratic parties would give priority to full-employment policies and welfare reforms, the trade unions would limit industrial conflict and co-operate in the economic growth policy, which alone permitted further social reform. Hibbs' correlations demonstrate not only that there is a mechanism linking low industrial conflict and a strong welfare commitment, but also that working-class organisations are somewhat more sensitive to its operation than some left-wing intellectuals.

Reformist socialists in Western Europe have noticed the existence of such a mechanism in Scandinavia, but have failed to understand the basic precondition of its operation. This precondition is that the working class should have a political instrumentality in whose commitments it can put its faith. As Walton and McKersie have pointed out in the context of industrial relations bargaining, the side that goes for a competitive strategy of attempting to take gains from the other side is risking the possibility of losing the greater benefits that might result from a co-operative strategy. On the other hand, the risk attached to a co-operative strategy is that there is no inherent guarantee that the other side will not adopt a competitive strategy and take all the gains for itself (Walton and McKersie, 1965). On a societal level, this is a vicious circle which vitiates the possibility of any genuine and lasting co-operation by working-class organisations in capitalist societies that are politically dominated by parties of the Right. Because the same dominant class has control of the political and economic processes, working-class organisations have no guarantee that, if they co-operate with management or attempt to fulfil 'national' economic policy objectives, it will be their members as well as the employers who gain. The brave hopes of each new incomes policy — each one only a revamped version of previous initiatives in inter-class co-operation — turn to dust and ashes of a return to free collective bargaining as trade unions begin to entertain justified doubts about the redistributional fairness of the gains or losses made by different sections of the community. However, if there is a political instrumentality which can be trusted by the working class to guarantee that a co-operative strategy will not be covertly transformed into a competitive zero-sum game, the possibility of trade unions entering into binding commitments to minimise strike activity and promote economic growth is much enhanced.[9] Under these circumstances, *and only under these circumstances*, can the vicious circles, normally inherent in the inter-class relationships of a capitalist society, be transformed for an appreciable period into the virtuous circles of class co-operation.

But it is clearly the case that the political instrumentality that is most likely to be trusted by the working class is a party whose declared aim is to promote working-class aims. In other words, in contradiction to the beliefs of reformist ideologues, a democratic socialist party which stresses its character as a class party is more likely to be able to function in such a way as to promote social harmony. A democratic socialist party which is to be trusted by the working class cannot see its role as a neutral arbiter of the national interest but must, instead, act as a counterweight to the entrenched economic power of capitalism. If trade unions are to co-operate in making 'the national cake grow bigger and bigger', they must have the assurance that they possess an agency which can punish the greed of capitalism.

It should be obvious that this depiction of the mechanism by which conflict is minimised in Scandinavia departs somewhat from the prevailing sociological orthodoxy regarding the institutionalisation of conflict in advanced industrial societies. Basically, the institutionalisation thesis rests on the assumption that common values and common interests are of greater salience than divergent economic and political interests. The argument presupposes that once social groups can arrive at compromises and in particular, elaborate sets of rules for making further compromises, all parties will see that they have more to gain from co-operation than from conflict. Once such rules have been institutionalised they become a *Deus ex machina* guaranteeing continuing social harmony. That institutional mechanisms for the accommodation of opposed interest can facilitate co-operation and lessen class tensions is demonstrated, not least, by the successful conduct of decision-making by means of corporate pluralism in Scandinavia. That they need not function in this way is shown by the persistence of industrial conflict in many nations with developed institutions of conflict resolution, Britain being an obvious example. It is, therefore, my contention that successful institutionalisation of conflict in industrial societies depends on the prior existence of a political guarantee that working class interests will receive consideration; it is not in itself such a guarantee.

The institutionalisation thesis is a misleading explanation of social processes in advanced industrial societies because it fails to suggest any reason why co-operation to procure common goals should produce greater gains for any given social group than co-operation *plus a redistributive strategy in its own favour.* Thus, there are only two options available to working-class organisations which wish a greater share in the rewards produced by the economic system. The first is to pursue a wholly redistributive strategy: 'to expropriate the expropriators'. This is the Marxist strategy. The second is the democratic socialist strategy, which rests on the possibility of gaining sufficient political power to guarantee that co-operation is not suborned to the detriment of the working class. This latter solution is not the Hobbesian one that men require 'a common power to keep then all in awe', for unless that power is manifestly not an instrumentality of the political Right, it cannot balance the power already inherent in capitalist control of the economy. By themselves, mechanisms of institutionalised conflict resolution simply lead to compromises perpetuating the already existing balance of social forces. That institutionalisation is not an adequate guarantor of the interests of workers, or wage earners in general, is demonstrated precisely by the higher levels of welfare state provision in those few countries which have had dominant democratic socialist parties based on strong working-class support.

It is important that the preceding argument is not read as implying that the socialist goal of an egalitarian society can be achieved purely by class co-operation. My contention is that such co-operation can only be advantageous to the working class when the dominant political force in society is either an agency of working-class interests as such or is, at least, quite explicitly not a creature of the political Right. There may well be inherent limitations to the degree of redistribution that can be procured by means of class co-operation, and it is most significant that the Scandinavian Social Democrats are, after many decades, tentatively adjusting their strategy towards a more frontal attack on the prerogatives of capital ownership. However, and this is the point I would wish to stress being a democratic socialist myself, the development of progressively more egalitarian and welfare-orientated Social Democratic image of society in Scandinavia permits some optimism that the trauma of even greater social change may not fundamentally affect human liberties and democratic rights.

Extensive welfare state provision is by no means the only way in which the working class has gained by inter-class co-operation in Scandinavia. Full employment is, as was stressed in chapter 1, another fundamental premise of labour movement solidarity in pursuit of economic growth. Indeed, it is an aspect of policy which has historical priority over welfare aims, since it was as the party of full employment that Social Democracy established the trust of the organised working class in the 1930s. The postwar situation is adequately summarised by Gruchy.

> In order to maintain its support among the workers who comprise the backbone of the Social Democratic party, the party has to keep the matter of what is of primary importance to the trade union members in the forefront of economic policy considerations — and of primary importance is a high level of employment. Any political party in the Scandinavian countries that would not assign a very high priority to full–employment policy would have a dim political future (Gruchy, 1966, p. 437).

The transition from the Social Democratic Party to any political party in this statement is a wholly accurate reflection of the way in which what started as a distinctive policy goal of Social Democracy has become a part of the prevailing image of society. This is not an example of some natural harmony of economic interests gradually making itself apparent. For the bourgeois parties a full-employment policy is a question of sheer survival. To the degree that they remain more suspect of having interests which may occasionally conflict with such a policy, it is necessary for them to maintain a stance that assures the electorate that it is not their intention to yield to such interests. The penalty for failure is electoral nemesis. The fact that the immediate reaction of the first bourgeois government in Sweden for over forty years to a declining economic situation was to borrow abroad to finance major inflationary measures is testimony enough to the operation of this particular aspect of the politics of virtuous circles.

Although a weaker economy and a lesser degree of labour movement solidarity have made full-employment policy more difficult to achieve in Denmark than elsewhere in Scandinavia, the great contrast is not between the Scandinavian countries but between them and Britain. The postwar history of the British labour movement illustrates precisely the vicious circles that are inherent in inter-class co-operation on terms dictated by a party of the Right. The historic role of the British Conservative Party has been as self-appointed interpreter of the national interest. The Party's justification for such a self-image is its cross-class appeal: its ability to attract the votes of the great majority of the middle class and a substantial minority of the working class. But, just as in Scandinavia, the dominant political class has given the national interest a particular slant and assimilated it as part of the Social Democratic image of society so, in Britain, the Conservative Party has left its own imprint on the national interest and made it merely an aspect of the Bourgeois image of society. Just as, in Scandinavia, the Social Democrats have defined the ground on which the political struggle takes place so, in Britain, the Conservative vision of the national interest provides the basic rules for permissable political conduct. The British labour movement can either work within the limits thus imposed and thereby undermine the solidarity of the labour movement, or it can promote working-class interests and be labelled as a sectional party working against the national interest. This dilemma facing the labour movement has been described by Butler and Stokes.

> The party's historic justification for existence was the improvement of the lot of the working class, especially the successive extensions of the welfare state. But Labour in power, or near it, has also had to face problems and formulate policies touching national goals and not simply the more sectional or parochial interests of class. It is indeed arguable that only by doing so could Labour have established its qualifications to govern in the eyes of a majority of the electorate, including a substantial part of the working class itself. Yet the conflict between national and sectional interests is sufficiently real for Labour to be drawn away by the tenure of power from a primary identification with class goals and to make the difference between the parties in these terms seem less sharp. The most notable example was the adoption by Labour Chancellors in the middle 1960s of economic policies that would heighten unemployment and lower the real incomes of working people in order to right the country's international balance of payments and defend the pound (Butler and Stokes, 1969, pp. 120-1).

My only disagreement would be with the last sentence for, surely the most notable example of the Labour Party or, at least, some of its leaders, sacrificing the working-class interest in full employment occurred as long ago as 1931! It should be emphasised once again that the dilemma of British democratic socialism is not something which can be readily resolved by conscious manipulation of the kind advocated by reformists. To compromise, in Britain, is to accept the definitions of reality of the Right, and not to compromise is either a recipe for electoral self-immolation or a declaration of revolutionary intent. Exactly the same situation of the national interest being rigged against democratic socialism exists in all countries with strong parties of the Right. One has only to think of German Social Democratic acquiescence, not to mention positive collaboration, in fashioning 'Emergency Laws' and a *'Berufsverbot'* to realise that it is not in Britain alone that democratic socialists are caught up in the politics of vicious circles.

The reciprocal interrelationship between the maintenance of Social Democratic political ascendancy, labour movement solidarity in pursuit of economic growth, and the achievement of the twin goals of full employment and enhanced welfare state provision is but one aspect of the politics of virtuous circles. It is, however, the aspect that should be stressed most strongly in comparative perspective, since the mechanism involved is that which most clearly distinguishes Scandinavian political life in the last four decades from that elsewhere, and which has functioned as the precondition of the more extensive social and economic co-operation that has characterised Scandinavian social organisation in the same period. As already noted in passing, the mechanisms of corporate pluralism are but rather elaborate versions of institutions of conflict resolution which exist elsewhere. Every modern nation has mechanisms which attempt to resolve industrial conflict, facilitate wage bargaining, reach price agreements, and regulate the myriad complex relationships of an advanced industrial society. However, although such institutions are universal, commentators have stressed their peculiar salience in Scandinavia.

The institutional mechanisms which exist to regulate conflict and promote co-operation between diverse social groups in Scandinavia do not achieve their success by blurring the distinctions between interests, but rather by emphasising them. Just as the party alignment is largely a reflection of the occupational cleavages within the Scandinavian societies, so the constellation of interest groups which bargain and negotiate within the corporate pluralist universe constitutes the organisational expression of the same balance of forces. As has been shown, the trade unions are but an arm of a united labour movement, which is strong precisely because it both gains the electoral support of a vast majority of working-class voters and acts as the representative of the industrial workers in the sphere of wage bargaining. The organisations of agricultural producers are closely linked to the farmers' parties, and derive their solidarity from the reliance of predominantly small to medium-sized agricultural enterprises on co-operative arrangements for marketing and distribution. Indeed, the farmers' parties of Norway and Sweden were originally created as the political instrumentality of the agricultural organisations. Employers' organisations and interest groups representing the views of the upper white-collar employees have a sympathetic hearing from Conservative parties, which gain much of their electoral support from these social strata. Solidarity is just as much the operational code amongst the higher social strata as amongst the lower. In Sweden and Denmark, it was the centralisation and unity of employers' organisations which initiated similar processes on the trade union side. As Galenson points out, the solidarity of Norwegian employers is no less.

> Norwegian employers view the ability of American trade unions to play one employer off against another with incredulity. It is highly unethical for a Norwegian employer to capitalize upon the labor trouble of a fellow employer by attempting to win away his trade, and any such effort is met with swift retribution (Galenson, 1970, p. 80).

In Scandinavia, the trade unions' power to 'black' strike-breakers is matched by the employers' willingness to boycott firms which undermine capitalist solidarity. In the context of upper white-collar organisation, it is notable that in Sweden, the country which has taken corporate pluralism to its ultimate lengths, there exists a strong central organisation covering all professions in which the minimum qualification is academic education. It may say something about the success of Social Democratic egalitarian policies in Sweden that the only occasion on which a postwar government has had to intervene directly in a labour dispute was when this organisation, together with a smaller interest group representing higher civil servants, went on strike because of declining wage differentials.

A corporate pluralist decision-making apparatus whose distinguishing feature is the salience of distinct interest cleavages manifests precisely the same paradox of class division resulting in social harmony that was noted as characteristic of the confrontation of a working-class party dominant in the political order and a capitalist class controlling the economic process. In effect, the corporate pluralist mechanism may be regarded as the organisational equivalent of the balance of political and economic forces in society. Corporate pluralism has deep historical roots in the Scandinavian political cultures, but the existence of mechanisms for expressing sectional opinions has been no guarantee of the accommodation of interests in the context of the class conflicts of an industrial society. As Hugh Heclo notes, royal commissions have been a regular part of the Swedish administrative process from early in the nineteenth century. Their tasks have been investigative, but have included a strong emphasis on consulting interested parties and, since the emergence of parliamentary politics, have increasingly included direct representation of legislators and interest groups (Heclo, 1974, p.43). Similar institutions have played an important role in policy formulation in both Denmark and Norway. However, despite numerous commissions which investigated the problem of the unemployed in the 1920s, they could do little more than recommend proposals for marginal improvements in the system of relief, since they accepted the economic orthodoxy that unemployment was a consequence of an excessive wage level. Similarly, neither the basic agreement between the Danish trade unions and employers in 1899 setting out rules for the conduct of disputes, nor the Labour Courts which were established in all the Scandinavian countries by the 1920s, had an appreciable effect on the level of industrial conflict. As has already been pointed out at some length, the decisive factor in diminishing the level of unemployment and the volume of strike activity was the assumption of office by the political arm of the labour movement.

However, in the context of the political guarantee provided by Social Democracy that working-class co-operation with other groups would not be undermined by the strength of the employers' economic position, it has been possible to transform the largely peripheral role of institutional mechanisms for conflict resolution into a major instrument of decision-making and administration. I have quoted Stein Rokkan's description of the Norwegian variant of corporate pluralism in a previous chapter, and Nils Andren makes a similar point in a Swedish context.

> Due to their exceptional strength, the organisations, especially the big trade unions, employers', consumers' and farmers' organizations, constitute a kind of extra-constitutional power balance system. When the parties in the system arrive at an agreement on some question, the matter is in reality generally decided (Andren, 1961, p. 20).

It is not simply their strength which leads to organised groups playing such a crucial role in Scandinavia, but also the fact that, where co-operation is not perverted to the particular advantage of one social class, organisations are a better locus for reaching genuine accommodations between the clearly defined interests of different social groups. They perform this role more effectively than political parties because the lines of division within the corporate universe are even more distinct than in the parliamentary arena; groups are only responsible to their own constituencies and, unlike parties, are not competing for each others'. Indeed, the extent to which the substance of politics is determined by inter-group compromises rather than by parliamentary conflict is probably a rather accurate measure of the degree to which inter-class co-operation is pursued within a mutually acceptable framework. Groups only resort to the political arena when either they feel that they are getting a raw deal or when their demands are greater than are compatible with other groups' vital interests. In recent years, there has been an increasing tendency for the trade unions to go outside the corporate universe to procure the industrial relations reforms they have demanded, and it has been the employers who have complained most vociferously about the alleged breakdown of the traditional system of group accommodation.

The corporate pluralist system has been the instrument by which working-class organisations have been politically integrated into the fabric of a capitalist society. Four decades of progressively increasing representation at every level and in every institutional sphere have made the trade unions not only the most powerful single veto group in society, but also amongst the most influential forces in defining the prevailing image of society. The precondition of that political integration, as of enhanced welfare state provision and full employment, has been the political dominance of Social Democracy in Scandinavia. But the final paradox is, of course, that political integration, enhanced welfare state provision and full employment have themselves been the preconditions of Social Democratic political dominance. Social Democratic attachment to working-class interests has been matched by working-class attachment to Social Democracy. Thus, Social Democratic political dominance, as much as enhanced welfare state provision, can be seen as the culmination of the politics of virtuous circles.

3.3 The weakness of the Right

A party system in which the working class is undivided and the Right is weak is the condition which has permitted Social Democratic reformism — the politics of virtuous circles — to be practiced successfully in Scandinavia. Weakness and strength are, of course, relative terms, and it would be absurd to suggest that the reformist strategies of democratic socialist parties in other nations had failed entirely. As I had occasion to point out, Britain has a remarkably good showing on the Index of Pure Welfare for a country whose Gross Domestic Product *per capita* is so low (see Table 2.5). But the limits to reformist policy in Britain are by now clearly evident. The possibility of mobilising labour movement solidarity to build a stronger economic base for further reform is negligible because the Labour Party necessarily works within the framework of ideas established by the dominant Bourgeois image of society. If one is more interested in outcomes than ideology — one's priority is the improvement of the condition of the working class rather than the success of the socialist movement — it is apparent that of two factors discussed, it is the weakness of the Right which is the most crucial. A comparison of Britain and the Netherlands establishes this point. The Netherlands, second only to Britain, makes the best showing on the Index of Pure Welfare relative to GDP *per capita*. But, in the absence of a strong Right, the working class, divided as it is on religious grounds, has had a guarantee that class co-operation in the 'national interest' would not be subverted to its disadvantage, and in consequence both the level of welfare and of economic growth have been much higher than in Britain. Presumably, it could be argued however, that there are better long-term prospects for the creation of an egalitarian society where working-class interests are expressed through a political instrumentality which is explicitly identified with those interests; in other words, through a socialist party. It is significant that in the decade in which Scandinavian Social Democracy has been tentatively searching for means of going beyond mere reformism, Dutch politics have been becoming more polarised, with the Labour Party deliberately and successfully challenging the religious fragmentation of the working class. The 'politics of accommodation' may be a functional alternative to the politics of democratic socialist reform, but it is an inadequate instrument for creating economic democracy, which is as much the goal of the Dutch Labour Party as of Scandinavian Social Democracy.

In one sense, the task that I set myself is completed, since both the dominance of the Scandinavian Social Democratic parties and the consequences of that dominance have now been explained. However, in this last section, I wish to address myself briefly to what is, in a way, the most fascinating problem of all: *why has the Scandinavian Right been so weak?* The discussion of the relationship between class and party in Scandinavia demonstrated the divisions of interest and traditional heritage between the bourgeois parties, and the earlier account of the growth of the Scandinavian labour movements showed that they were subject to only the most limited state-imposed restrictions on their freedom to organise. Moreover, the advance towards democratisation and the later socialist assumption of office were resisted by the Right, but never to the point where violence was preferred to concession on the least disadvantageous terms possible at the time. This has been by no means the most common pattern in recent European history. The Right in the majority of the continental European countries not infrequently resorted to violence and administrative oppression in its struggle to prevent the victory of the masses and, even in Britain, the epitomy of peaceful political development, the barriers to working-class organisation were much greater than in Scandinavia. To attempt to answer the question of why the Scandinavian Right has been so much weaker than comparable parties elsewhere in Europe is to provide an historical dimension to the explanation of Social Democratic ascendancy in Scandinavia.

It is, however, the type of question which many contemporary political scientists, fearing simultaneously the Scylla of ideographic explanation and the Charybdis of infinite historical regression, avoid altogether, creating as an alternative the construct of 'political culture' as a means of papering over the cracks. Clearly, political culture is an important concept, but it is a particularly dangerous one in an historical context where survey data is unavailable and there is a not inconsiderable risk that the evidence from which the concept is derived will be precisely that which the concept is later called upon to explain. Thus, there is sometimes a tendency to explain the yielding nature of the Scandinavian Right in terms of cultural traditions of political accommodation which are, in turn, illustrated by prior manifestations of the yielding nature of the Right. Historiography of the more popular ilk sometimes falls into the same trap, as is demonstrated by the following explanation of the peculiarly peaceful nature of Danish political development.

> Revolutions in Denmark have a habit of taking place in their own special way. In 1660, when absolute monarchy was introduced, the King merely had a talk with some of the leading men in the country and then announced that from then on there would be absolute monarchy — and that was all. In 1848 there was unrest all over Europe. Shots were ringing out in the streets of Berlin and Paris. In Denmark, feelings mounted to such extraordinary heights that a number of honest citizens donned their top hats and frock coats, went to see the King, and told him from now on they wanted a free constitution. They got it! (Lauring, 1968, p. 211).

The question remains: why do revolutions in Denmark have a habit of taking place in a special way?[10] What is the simplest of fallacies in historiography is seemingly the operative principle of many of those political scientists who preface their studies of particular countries by the compulsory chapter on the historical and cultural heritage. Political culture becomes a residual category into which the author dumps all those problems which he is either unwilling or unable to explain. But every nation does have its own unique historical and cultural heritage. To understand its impact on contemporary politics requires not merely an account of cultural attitudes, but an explanation of the structural *milieu* in which they arose and the structures and institutions which perpetuate their influence.

In a way, a residual category like political culture is a natural enough subsidiary concept to be developed in the context of the sort of over-arching theory that has characterised the sociological approach to politics in the last two decades. For a theoretical edifice, which conceived the development of all modern societies proceeding from an ineluctable functional logic grounded in the very process of industrialisation, it served the useful purpose of explaining away the supposedly minor variations which did exist.[11] However, any theoretical structure which is so general as to leave no room for the manifestation of historical diversity is thereby necessarily condemned to sterility, not to mention empirical falsification. It is the recognition of this point which makes Ralf Dahrendorf reject the relevance of any generalised notion of an 'industrial society' in attempting to understand the nature of political development. This view is put forward in the context of his discussion of the causes of the failure of liberal-democracy in Germany.

> Germany turned into an industrial country without thereby becom- ing any more similar to England than she was before. Industrializa- tion has not led to rendering German and French, French and American, American and Japanese society more alike, unless one sees, with the superficial perception of the cultural pessimist, like- ness and levelling in the simple fact that there are, in all these countries, foundries, cities, tractors and cans (Dahrendorf, 1967, p. 47).

The dissimilarity of industrial societies leads Dahrendorf to the con- clusion that social structures and cultural attitudes generated by such universal forces as industrialism are inevitably drawn into a particular historical context and are assimilated in a manner peculiar to it alone. The distinctiveness of Scandinavian political development which has culminated in dominant Social Democratic parties faced by weak and accommodating parties of the Right is further evidence of the same phenomenon. Whilst the existence of mass working-class parties is every- where closely related to changes in the social structure brought about by industrialisation and social mobilisation, the very much more diverse patterns displayed by non-socialist groupings in Western political systems are, at least, a partial reflection of the interest cleavages in the pre-industrial social structure. These cleavages are made relevant to con- temporary political life by their crystallisation in party alignments during the period of democratisation and by their impact on the pre- vailing image of society.

Two aspects of the development of the Scandinavian social structures in the nineteenth century seem to have been decisive in leading to the emergence of a weak and accommodating party of the Right. The first was the unusually strong position of the independent peasantry which gave a distinctive cast to interest cleavages in societies in which political mobilisation was increasing. The second was the lateness of industriali- sation, which ensured that the peasantry had an entrenched position in the institutional structure before the appearance of new social forces, and the rapidity with which that industrialisation took place, which prevented the peasantry assuming a conservative stance prior to the growth of mass working-class organisations. Although the role of the peasantry and the impact of industrialisation have been topics which have recently received much attention from scholars whose concern has been to emphasise dissimilarities among the Scandinavian countries, the singularity of Scandinavian political development with respect to the joint impact of these factors appears clearly in comparative perspective.[12]

To restrict the focus to nineteenth-century Scandinavia is not to contest the validity of recent attempts to seek the origins of modern political forms in the organisation of early rural social structure and its adaptation to the imperatives of commercial or capitalist agriculture.[13] However, before the nineteenth century, the Scandinavian countries were characterised by markedly divergent agrarian and political structures. In terms of the historical evolution of the peasantry, two differentiating factors appear to be crucial. The greater peripherality of Sweden in the European state system, and the fact that under Swedish conditions the peasant was as important as a warrior as he was as a producer of economic surplus, gave the Swedish peasantry a degree of political influence unrivalled elsewhere in Scandinavia, or, indeed, anywhere else in Europe (Castles, 1973, pp. 313-31). Already by the seventeenth century, the Swedish peasantry were represented as a fourth Estate in the *Riksdag* and, by the time of the nineteenth-century conflicts over the reform of this parliamentary institution, had a veto power over constitutional change. On the other hand, the fact that large-scale manorial farming was only possible in Denmark and the southern part of Sweden meant that in much of Sweden (before 1809, Finland was an integral part of Sweden) and, particularly in Norway, the peasantry retained their economic independence. Thus, early peasant freedom in both Sweden and Norway were closely related to the weakness of an agricultural infrastructure which made the exploitation of peasant labour largely unprofitable. In contrast, until the latter part of the eighteenth century, the Danish peasantry resembled their counterparts in much of eastern Europe in terms of lack of independence and legal subordination.

However, from 1788 onward the more liberal outlook of the urban bourgeoisie, which had become a powerful influence in the Danish absolutist state, led to the transformation of the medieval village community by the emancipation of the peasantry and the gradual transition from copyhold to freehold tenure. These changes, together with the growing importance of the enclosure movement, which, having begun in Denmark, spread first to Sweden and somewhat later to Norway, tended to make the rural social structures of the Scandinavian countries progressively more similar. As Øyvind Østerud argues:

The individual family farm became the basic unit in the agricultural pattern all over Scandinavia, in sharp contrast to the British enclosures, which rather stimulated the final elimination of the peasantry as a social formation. Scandinavian enclosure occurred *at a time when there was no population outlet in industrial work* — as had been the case in Britain — and it furthered farm partition and increased peasant farming rather than the abolition of peasant land. Large-scale farming on the English model had never become so dominant in Scandinavia, and enclosure therefore had very dissimilar effects. There was no mass of dispossessed village labourers to be drained off the land, but rather a substantial amount of peasant leaseholders who acquired individualized freehold (Østerud, 1974, p. 184. My italics).[14]

This contrast between Britain and Scandinavia makes very clear how different could be the impact of a reform designed to increase agricultural productivity in the context of societies at different stages of economic development. In pre-industrial Scandinavia, enclosure fostered the emergence of a distinct class of independent peasant proprietors with small- to medium-sized holdings, whereas, in Britain, there was a rapid shift of landless labourers to the burgeoning industrial centres. Moreover, the distinctiveness of the Scandinavian countries appears in even sharper relief if the focus of comparison is with Prussia and other areas in eastern Europe where a landowning aristocracy maintained a 'labour repressive' agricultural system in which the peasantry was tied to the land by quasi-feudal obligations (Moore, 1966, p. 435).[15]

Although the Swedish peasantry already possessed an institutionalised voice in the Fourth Estate, it was the Norwegian peasantry whose economic influence was first translated into a recognisably modern form of political representation. Under the mobilising pressures of the national crisis attendant on the separation from Denmark, the composition of the Eidsvold constitutional convention of 1814 nicely reflected the balance of power at the time. Of 112 delegates, 'fifty-nine members held office in the civil administration, the armed forces, or the church; thirty-seven belonged to the landholding peasantry . . . and eighteen were merchants or estate-owners' (Derry, 1973, p. 7). Although Norway came under the control of the Swedish Crown for the remainder of the nineteenth century, its parliamentary structure remained that formulated at Eidsvold, and accorded suffrage rights to 'all independent farmers and peasants who had leased a farm for at least five years' (Kuhnle, 1975, p. 17). Parliamentary representation was necessarily slower in coming in Denmark where the absolute monarchy persisted until 1848, but the national sentiments aroused by the subsequent war with Prussia led to the institution of what was, at the time, Europe's most liberal constitution. All men over the age of thirty, who were neither paupers nor servants living in their master's household, were accorded the right to vote in elections to both chambers of parliament and, although a conservative reaction resulted in a change of qualifications for the upper house electorate in 1866, the peasantry had a strong base for political agitation in the lower house. In Sweden, change was retarded by the absence of any national crisis to mobilise opinion and by the already established incorporation of the peasant stratum in the Estate system. However, the bicameral reform, which eventually took place in 1866, gave 20 per cent of the adult male population the vote for representatives in the new second chamber and, of 190 members elected in 1876, no less than 114 were peasant proprietors (Verney, 1957, pp. 190-1). Thus, in each of the Scandinavian countries, the independent peasantry had achieved substantial political incorporation before the advent of full-scale industrialisation.

The economic and political importance of the independent peasantry in the nineteenth century was partly cause and partly consequence of the equally atypical development of the aristocratic and patrician class. In Norway, an indigenous aristocracy had virtually disappeared by the end of the fourteenth century and, when the Constitution of 1814 was written, the idea of an upper house representing the privileged was decisively rejected. In 1821, the Norwegian parliament abolished all orders of nobility. In Sweden and Denmark, from the seventeenth century onward the aristocracy had been progressively transformed into a royal urban bureaucracy, many of whose members were more dependent on their incomes from office-holding than on revenues derived from landed estates. Presumably, the weak agricultural basis of the Scandinavian aristocracies was a consequence of the relatively poor opportunities for creating an economic surplus from the peasantry in countries in which agrarian production on a commercial scale only gradually became viable from the late eighteenth century. Throughout the nineteenth century it was the aristocratic and patrician class which formed the cabinets (until 1884 in Norway), civil bureaucracies and policy-formulating bodies in Scandinavia. The fact that this class was primarily urban in both location and cultural values, and that their influence was grounded more in service to the monarch than in independent ownership of land, gave it a weak basis for resistance to movements aiming at the democratisation of the polity. Demographic factors may also have been involved to some extent, with aristocracies, superimposed on a small population base and isolated on the European periphery, finding it difficult to regenerate their strength from within. The Swedish nobility was certainly unstable in demographic terms, and, of 3,000 noble lineages between 1280 and 1866, the majority died out with one-third surviving only a generation and very few more than four generations (Keller, 1963, pp. 229-31). This biological vulnerability of the aristocracy made it necessary to constantly renew aristocratic strength from outside, and there was a tendency for some intergenerational mobility to take place between peasantry and nobility (Carlsson, 1962). Its main avenue was for the sons of peasants to enter the Church, and for their children to enter the ranks of the noble bureaucracy by virtue of higher education, which was established as the primary criterion for office-holding in the Scandinavian countries appreciably earlier than was general in the rest of Europe. In Norway, where there was no aristocratic class this 'tendency to co-opt new elements' was even more pronounced as a consequence of 'the weakness of ascriptive values in the civil servant upper class' (Torgersen, 1970, p. 103).

The main line of cleavage in the Scandinavian social structures, before the appearance of an appreciable industrial sector in the late nineteenth century, was between the economic and cultural interests of the rural independent peasantry and the urban aristocratic bureaucracy. The emphasis of peasant protest was somewhat different in each country, with the Norwegian movement putting the greatest stress on a distinct peasant cultural identity opposed to the values and alien civilisation of the towns, and the Danish movement focusing on the economic struggle with 'the capitalistic aristocracy of town and country' (Hovde, 1943, p. 551). Although somewhat less intense in manifestation, peasant politicisation in Sweden emphasised both cultural and economic separateness from the towns. In all three countries, peasant identity was expressed through the growth of 'popular movements' promoting religious fundamentalism, temperance values, and agricultural co-operation. In Norway, the divergence between Danish, which was the common language of the towns, and the rural vernacular gave rise to a strong peasant-orientated movement for language reform. Gradually, cultural and economic protest became linked with political demands for the further widening of the franchise and the institution of parliamentary regimes. Thus, peasant separateness became enshrined in the basic fabric of the 'Left' parties which emerged to challenge the political privilege of the urban 'Right'.

The pattern of interest cleavages in Scandinavia clearly distinguishes its pattern of political development from that which occurred in Britain. As Rokkan points out, the divergent patterns of cleavage became crystallised in party alignments.

> This contrast in political development clearly did not reflect a difference in the salience of any *single* line of cleavage but a difference in the *joint* operation of two sets of cleavages: the opposition between the central nation-building culture and the traditions of the periphery, and the opposition between the primary and secondary

sectors of the economy. In Britain the central culture was upheld
and reinforced by a vast network of *landed* families, in the Nordic
countries by an essentially *urban* elite of officials and patricians. In
Britain the two cleavage lines *cut across* each other; in Scandinavia
they *reinforced* each other. The British structure encouraged a
gradual merger of urban and rural interests, while the Scandinavian
made for division and opposition. . . . The British Conservative Party
was able to establish a joint front of landed and industrial owner
interests, while the Scandinavian 'Right' remained essentially urban
and proved unable to establish any durable alliance with the Agrarians and the peripheral 'Left'. (Rokkan, 1970, p. 120.)

Herein lies the reason for the fundamental contrast between the strong
party of the Right which characterises British politics and the weakness
of the Right in Scandinavia. Cross-cutting cleavages in Britain gradually
facilitated the coalescence of the pre-industrial, landowning class, whose
wealth was based on large-scale commercial agriculture, and the urban
bourgeoisie on terms which at first perpetuated the *noblesse oblige*
image of society, but which allowed its slow, but ineluctable, permeation
by a capitalist ethic. Interests remained distinct through much of the
nineteenth century, but the shift in priorities toward a Bourgeois image
of society is already clearly marked by 1834, when the Speenhamland
system of outdoor relief for the poor gave way to 'the workhouse test'
and 'the principle of less eligibility', a change in orientation which was
blessed with the support of majorities of both Whigs and Tories in
the Reformed Parliament. By the end of the century, territorial representation, which was the expression of the rural-urban cleavage, had
been superseded by national politics initiated by a Conservative Party
based on the final merger of landed interests with urban and suburban
interests.

A similar coalescence of urban and rural interests was ruled out by
the superimposition of cultural and economic cleavages in the Scandinavian countries. The parties of the 'Left' opposed the urban 'Right',
both in order to assert the economic interests of small peasant producers against the priorities of a bureaucracy that was nurturing a fledg-
ling industry under its protective wing, and to affirm the distinctiveness
of its cultural values. In the course of the struggle for democratisation,
the 'Left' forged an alliance with urban and peripheral radicals, but
even this unity of opposition to the 'Right' across the urban-rural divide
could not survive intact once the immediate objective was achieved, and
the subsequent separation out of distinct Liberal and Agrarian parties
(agrarian Liberal and Radical-Liberal in Denmark) made for further
fragmentation of non-socialist forces in the early decades of this century.

Whereas in Britain, the politics of territorial division was overcome by a nationally based Conservative Party, in Scandinavia:

> The move toward nationalized politics was essentially a consequence of the spread of the Social Democrats from the cities to the rural areas and the alliance of the industrial working class and the rural proletariat (Rokkan, 1970, p. 241).

It has already been noted that, in Britain, it is the Conservative Party which serves to interpret the nature of the 'national interest', whereas in the Scandinavian countries this role is played by the Social Democratic parties. This contrast can now be seen to have deep historical roots in the interest cleavages of the respective social structures.

In this brief and schematic account of the main features of the nineteenth-century Scandinavian social structures, no mention has been made of one of the protagonists which would have featured centrally in the discussion of a similar period elsewhere in Western Europe: the bourgeoisie. Generally, that is because the failure to commercialise agriculture to any considerable degree before the conclusion of the eighteenth century in Denmark, and some decades later in Sweden and Norway, meant the retardation of industry and urban growth and with them the urban bourgeoisie. By 1850 only Denmark had a sizeable urban sector and evidence of widespread support for liberal *laissez-faire* doctrines. In Norway and Sweden, the advent of a numerically substantial class of industrial entrepreneurs had to wait until the industrial take-off in the last two decades of the century and, in the meanwhile, the conservative oligarchs, in whose hands rested political authority, were more mindful of peasant prerogatives voiced in parliament than of the assertion of liberal economic ideas. Such ideas were too powerful to be wholly ignored, but they were frequently subtly transmogrified in such a way as not to conflict with traditional corporate conceptions stressing the importance of the community rather than the individual. Thus, in Sweden, as early as 1844, one could find an eminent liberal, Erik Gustaf Geijer, arguing that unbridled competition led to a society which operated according to the principle of 'might makes right', and the need for freedom of association to ensure that there were strong groups which could protect the individual.[16] Moreover, the conservative bureaucratic elite had no inherent ideological preference for individualism at the expense of the community's welfare, and Torgersen suggests that in Norway, at least, liberal ideas were more honoured in the breach than the observance.

> [The] upper class was largely composed of public officials, civil servants, who because of their very position, had a high degree of

good will towards public activity. And if they generally supported laissez-faire philosophy, they applied it with moderation if at all (Torgersen, 1974, p. 203).

Clearly, too, although the liberal theory of representation was to spread throughout Scandinavia during the nineteenth century, this was less by the disappearance of earlier institutional practices designed to provide a hearing for important sections of the community, but rather by their incorporation into the framework of the parliamentary system as was, for instance, the case with the general Scandinavian use of investigatory royal commissions.

Of course, part of the liberal doctrine was the destruction of the old guild organisations which had provided a collective voice for the small urban population of skilled craftsmen. This occurred in Scandinavia, but the reluctance of the authorities to accept the logical implications of their own actions is seen in the Swedish legislation of 1846, which, having promulgated the end of the guilds, stipulated that: 'Instead in every city, craftsmen who pay taxes will belong to a craft association dedicated to promoting that craft and protecting the interests of its members' (Article III, para. 1). In Denmark, guilds were abolished in theory in 1849, but in fact in 1862. Thereafter, the growth of craft associations and its tolerance by the authorities seems to have owed a great deal to a similar reluctance to abolish traditional channels of political access and communication.

The implication of the rather weak development of the urban bourgeoisie and the uncongeniality of liberal doctrines to elements of the bureaucracy was that the Bourgeois image of society, stressing unfettered economic individualism which was the dominant ethos in Britain throughout much of the nineteenth century, was to occur much later and be much less pervasive in its Scandinavian manifestation. The impact varied, however, with Denmark as an entrepot nation exposed earlier to new economic ideas and, perhaps, more susceptible to them in virtue of its historical experience of a relatively less egalitarian rural social structure than elsewhere in Scandinavia.[17] It is probable that the ultimate significance of the lag in the diffusion of liberal economic ideas to the European periphery would have been less had not industrialisation, when it came, been comparatively rapid, or if it had involved the destruction of the landed peasantry as a structural precondition. But in Sweden and Norway industrial take-off only seriously got under way by the 1880s, leaving only a minor potential for bourgeois cultural imperatives to reshape the prevailing image of society prior to the assumption of a major political role by the Social Democrats in the early decades of the twentieth century. Industrialisation was somewhat more gradual in Denmark, and it has been precisely in that part of Scandi-navia that Social Democratic dominance has been least secure. In Sweden and Norway, it was largely the import of foreign capital, rather than the extraction of an economic surplus from the peasantry, which financed industrial take-off, and in Denmark it was a turn to animal husbandry of a kind particularly appropriate to the preservation of small- and medium-scale peasant proprietorship. Despite the somewhat more deve-loped bourgeoisie in Denmark, the peasantry there, as elsewhere in Scandinavia, survived until the end of the nineteenth century as the major economic and political bulwark against the possible usurpation of influence by an alliance of the conservative bureaucracy and the emergent urban magnates. By the last years of the century, the 'Left' parties of the peasant periphery had been joined in the struggle for de-mocratisation by the representatives of the organised working class: the Social Democratic parties.

In this process of political and social development there were pre-served a set of cultural attitudes and associated institutional practices not radically unassimilable to the ideas of modern socialism. In part, these were a carry over from the peasant egalitarianism which had existed in Norway and large parts of Sweden but, much more important, they were the heritage bequeathed by the oligarchic elites. For, as Samuel Beer has pointed out in a British context, old conservative conceptions, based on traditions of strong government, paternalism and the organic society, have far more in common with socialist collectivism than have either with the Bourgeois image of society stressing individualism and economic competition (Beer, 1965, pp. 69-71). The relative failure of the Bourgeois image of society in Scandinavia is the basic determinant of the willingness of elites to adapt and compromise with the ever-growing assertion of Social Democratic influence. Elsewhere in Europe, Social Democracy has had to fight a battle on two fronts: against the principle of individualism and against the pragmatic interest in differen-tial reward. Much of the failure on the latter front can be attributed to the draining of energy caused by the unending conflicts with the tenets of economic liberalism. Only in Scandinavia have the Social Democrats been fighting battles on a ground of their own choosing rather than tilt-ing at the ideological windmills of an outworn liberalism. Only in Scan-dinavia do the capitalists oppose Social Democracy on grounds of interest rather than principle, and since the Social Democrats have, *hitherto*, adopted a strategy which has ensured that their primary interest in main-taining reasonably profitable enterprises has not been sacrificed, but rather limited to 'the pleasant face of capitalism', that opposition has not in recent decades been markedly strident.

Notes

Chapter 1 The political dominance of Social Democracy

1 The others were the Australian Labor Party in 1910 and 1914, the Swedish Social Democratic Party in 1940 and 1968 and the Maltese Labour Party in 1945.

2 The nearness of the German Social Democrats to the 40 per cent barrier prior to the 1960s is not apparent from the averages presented in Table 1.1, but in the 1912 Reich election they polled 34.8 per cent and in 1919, 37.9 per cent.

3 The Danish Social Democrats polled 42.9 per cent in 1939 and 44.5 in 1943 in an election held despite the German occupation. The last election before the war, in 1936, gave the Norwegian Labour Party 46.7 per cent of the poll. There were two elections in Sweden during the war. In the 1940 election, the Social Democrats polled 53.8 per cent, and in 1944, 46.5 per cent.

4 I have deliberately restricted the comparison to European democratic socialist parties. However, the three cases which fall outside Europe exactly confirm the analysis to date. Between 1946-69, the average electoral support of the Australian Labor Party was 46.21 per cent. Accepting Sartori's view that the Liberal-Country Party is not a mere coalition but a 'coalescence' (Sartori, 1976, p. 188), the average margin of relative dominance for the ALP was −0.5 per cent. On that basis, or rather on the basis of the permanent over-representation of the rural areas in which the Country Party was strong, the ALP spent three years in office out of twenty four. In New Zealand, Labour averaged 45.48 per cent of the vote in the same period, and has a margin of relative dominance of −2 per cent. It was fortunate enough to spend six years in office. Once again, the result is exactly as in Britain and Austria: *the competition of two more or less similar sized parties is extremely unfavourable to democratic socialism.* Finally, the Israel Labour Party (Mapai) averaged 37.28 per cent (including Ma'arach in 1969) between 1949-69. Mapai has been the natural party of government since Israel's independence, and it does not seem wholly coincidental that the party's average margin of relative dominance has

been +21 per cent. On the whole, I would concur with Sartori's view (pp. 151-5) that Israel is in too many ways an extraordinary case to be included in comparative analysis, but it is interesting that the only democratic socialist party outside Scandinavia to exhibit a high level of relative dominance has been also a natural party of government.

5 This account is very dependent on W. L. Lafferty's *Economic Development and the Response of Labor in Scandinavia*, 1971, pp. 113-65.

6 There is sometimes a tendency for inter-Scandinavian comparisons to over-emphasise the precocity and gradualness of Danish development. According to Peter Flora the degree of urbanisation in Denmark in 1850 was 9 per cent, in Sweden 3.4 per cent, but in England and Wales 35 per cent (Flora, 1973, p. 242).

7 Nils Elvander has pointed out that there are severe psychological disadvantages to the collective affiliation of a large number of trade unionists, some of whom may not even be aware that they are technically members. He reports that in 1973, 23 per cent of the LO affiliated members of the Swedish Social Democratic Party voted for the bourgeois parties (Elvander, 1977, p. 13).

8 This 'September Agreement' predates similar agreements on the procedures to be adopted in industrial conflicts in Norway in 1935 and Sweden in 1938. It is interesting in the light of how often these latter agreements are interpreted as the basis of subsequent labour peace in Norway and Sweden that the 'September Agreement' was followed by three decades of bitter industrial conflict. As I shall later argue it is much more convincing to see labour peace as a concomitant of Social Democratic government.

9 See Olson, Jr., 1963, pp. 529-52, Lipset, 1963, pp. 27-63, and Kornhauser, 1959, pp. 153-4.

10 Infinitely the most sophisticated discussion of the relationship between economic development and labour radicalism in Scandinavia is to be found in Lafferty, 1971. He argues that, whilst at the level of aggregate economic growth, the supposed relationship may not hold, there are reasons for believing that it may contribute to an explanation at the ecological level. However, he also suggests the importance of political factors, and my own simplified presentation owes a great deal to his views.

11 Before 1905 the electoral system was indirect. The system adopted in that year involved the second ballot, and required an absolute majority on the first to secure election.

12 This assessment is attributed to the Minister of the Marine. See Tilton, 1974, p. 568.

13 The qualification 'virtual' is to cover the three months Agrarian Party caretaker government in Sweden in the summer of 1936 and one month bourgeois interregnum resulting from the Norwegian Labour Party's defeat over the King's Bay incident.

14 Apart from Rokkan's seminal essay, the Norwegian system is outlined in Kvavik, 1976. The Danish Interest group scene is surveyed in Laux, 1963. Corporatist tendencies in Sweden have been frequently the subject of comment, and a recent treatment is to be found in Ruin, 1974, pp. 171-84. A general discussion of corporate pluralism in the Scandinavian countries is to be found in Castles, 1977.

15 For a first-rate, up-to-date introduction to the major features of such co-operation in the Swedish context, see Forsebäck, 1976.

16 LO's role in initiating a wide range of departures in Swedish domestic policy since 1945 is discussed by Hancock, 1976. In this paper presented to the American Political Science Association meeting in Chicago, Hancock contrasts

the innovative stance of the Swedish trade unions with the far more passive record of the German Federation of Labour.

17 For two interesting accounts of Swedish labour market policy, see Öhman, 1974 and Mukherjee, 1972.

18 Unfortunately, it is quite impossible to make statistical comparisons of the levels of unemployment in the different Scandinavian countries. Whilst the Norwegian and Swedish figures relate to the percentage of unemployed wage earners in the total working population, the Danish figure is a percentage of 'the wage earners who are members of a state-recognized unemployment fund; these members amount to approximately half of all wage earners aged above 18' (Kuhlmann, 1974, p. 60). It is generally agreed that the Danish basis of calculation exaggerates the degree of unemployment experienced in comparison with the other Scandinavian countries. However, there is equal agreement that Denmark's unemployment record has been appreciably worse than Norway's or Sweden's in the postwar period.

19 The alignments within and between parties on the issue of the Nordic Defence Pact are chronicled in Barbara Haskel, 1976, pp. 76-85.

20 The use of the phrase 'red cabinet' is reported by Thomas, 1977, p. 252. My account of the emergence of the Danish Socialist People's Party is largely derived from this source.

21 The Gallup poll for March 1977 reported 5.5 per cent support for the Socialist Electoral Alliance and 43.7 per cent for the Labour Party. Data for the 1973 election are to be found in Table 1.4 of this chapter. I hope to be able to include the 1977 election results in this table at proof-stage, thereby giving the reader the opportunity to test the validity of my prediction.

22 The genuineness of bourgeois party assertions of a commitment to social welfare reforms will be doubted by readers of a left-wing persuasion. This subject is discussed in much greater detail in chapter 2 but, lest such readers feel inclined to abandon the argument at this point, I would point out that extensive social reform is not necessarily incompatible with the effective pursuit of private profit.

23 Apart from the type of economic factors mentioned in the text, there has been discussion of ideological and attitudinal dimensions of Progress Party support (Nielson, 1976, pp. 147-55) and also the impact on the electorate of a changing structure of political communication (Sauerberg, 1976, pp. 157-63). Any adequate account of the recently exhibited phenomenal ability of new parties in Denmark to obtain parliamentary representation should also point to the very low threshold to representation in the Danish electoral system. In this respect, Denmark shares important similarities with the Netherlands, which has also experienced intense party fragmentation in the last decade.

24 Comparisons of the incidence of taxation in different countries are notoriously unsatisfactory because of the varying components included under similar rubrics, and because of the widely divergent methods of financing social security schemes. Nevertheless, the following breakdown of state taxes into indirect and other (largely income) taxes does give some indication of the degree to which the Danish system differs from that of the other Scandinavian countries.

Date: 1973	Denmark %	Norway %	Sweden %
Indirect taxes	52.67	68.45	65.42
Other taxes	47.32	31.54	34.57

Source: *Yearbook of Nordic Statistics 1975,* p. 230.

25 Part of that strategy, as it has emerged in the discussions leading up to the adoption of the Party's manifesto for its 1977 Congress, has been the idea of 'economic democracy'. This concept will be discussed in the next chapter, but the basic aim is to promote greater social and economic equality by setting up wage earners' funds to share in the rights and rewards accruing to industrial ownership. It is clear that the Social Democrats see this not merely as a means of socialist advance, but also as a means of establishing better relationships with the trade unions.

Chapter 2 Equality and welfare in capitalist society

1 On the question of social mobility via the mechanism of enhanced educational opportunity, it should be pointed out that Parkin's 'agnosticism' becomes rather dubious. In the context of advanced capitalist societies, he argues that educational mobility is meritocratic rather than egalitarian and 'is perfectly compatible with a modern capitalist order' (p. 123). However, in discussing the problem of classes in Socialist societies (i.e., Eastern Europe), he points out that, whilst from a synchronic perspective, there is a genuine barrier between the 'new class' of the white-collar intelligentsia and *apparatchiki* and the rest of society,

> If we take a diachronic view of the same system we are bound to note that this boundary is a highly permeable one in the sense that movement into the 'new class' from below is continually taking place. Seen from this angle the 'classlessness' thesis has greater plausibility (p. 158).

A real agnostic would, surely, ask: how is it that intergenerational mobility in Communist societies suggests the plausibility of classlessness, whereas precisely the same phenomenon in capitalist societies is conducive to the more efficient operation of the capitalist order?

2 Each sample was drawn from a single factory in the engineering industry. The sample universe in each case was manual workers aged between 25 and 54. In the Swedish case, this gave a total of 141 potential respondents of whom 122 participated. In the British case, it gave a total of 528 respondents of whom 176 were asked to participate, and 128 finally co-operated. Having discussed the composition of these samples, Scase suggests: 'If then, the opinions of the samples cannot be regarded as representative of those of the more general populations they can, at least, be seen as *indicative* of them' (Scase, 1977, p. 93. Italics in original). The problem is, of course, to know in what ways they are indicative of them!

3 I want to make it clear that I am not trying to say that Communist and democratic socialist ideologies are so different that comparison is impossible. The problem is one of devising an initial taxonomy of ideologies of a kind which can make comparison fruitful. As Giovanni Sartori points out: 'If two or more items are identical, we do not have a problem of comparability. On the other hand, if two or more items have nothing, or not enough in common, we rightly say that stones and rabbits cannot be compared. By and large then, we obtain comparability when two or more items appear "similar enough", that is neither identical nor utterly different' (Sartori, 1970, p. 1035). It is Wilensky, who, by subsuming democratic socialist and Communist ideologies under a single measure of 'planning for equality', suggests that these ideologies are sufficiently similar to raise no problem of comparability.

4 Two points should be noted. First, Wilensky advances such structural explanations only to explain that part of welfare diversity which is not already explained by economic development, age of the welfare system and age of the population. Second, Wilensky does not say that the comparison is of the rich countries of the West, but rather of all twenty-two nations in the sample. It would be pedantic to calculate the incidence of references to Czechoslovakia, East Germany and the USSR but, suffice it to say, they appear underrepresented on a statistical basis.

5 A presentation of the Swedish study is to be found in Sten Johansson, 1973.

6 It should be noted that many scholars overcome this problem by studying the data *rather than the real world*. This strategy removes all difficulties except that of understanding why they bother to do research in the first place.

7 According to the *Yearbook of Nordic Statistics 1975*, p. 245, the figures for 1966 were (percentages):

    Denmark: 13.7   Norway: 11.6   Sweden: 13.6

For 1973, they were (percentages):

    Denmark: 21.0   Norway: 18.6   Sweden: 20.9

Interestingly, Wilensky's data for 1966, although basically similar in the Danish and Norwegian instances, differ radically in the Swedish case. According to his figures, derived from ILO, *The Cost of Social Security, 1964-6, 1972*, the 1966 data should read (percentages):

    Denmark: 13.9   Norway: 12.6   Sweden: 17.5

This makes clear a fourth common feature of much comparative work; namely, error. It is not clear why this discrepancy between ILO and Nordic Council material should exist, but it seems inherently probable that the Nordic Council data provide a more accurate inter-Scandinavian comparison, since they include the same components of social security expenditure for each country.

8 There are five countries which depart markedly from the relationship which one might expect to hold between high government revenue and a low infant mortality rate. They are Germany and Austria, which manifest high levels of government revenue and high infant mortality rates, and Japan, Spain and Switzerland, which exhibit an opposite pattern. The relevant data for both variables are OECD figures for 1974, which are presented in the text below. Russett's data for 1960 confirm the findings for Germany and Austria, but suggest either that Japan and Spain have experienced a miraculous improvement in health care in the intervening period, or that somebody's data is at fault (Russett *et al*, 1964, pp. 200-1). Russett's data also confirm the finding for Switzerland.

9 'Welfare effort' and 'welfare output' are terms introduced by Wilensky, 1975, p. 17.

10 The degree of dispersion for each variable expressed as a percentage of the highest value is as follows: general government revenue: 43.77, public spending on education: 48.75, GDP *per capita*: 54.07 and infant mortality: 59.14.

11 For a discussion of the similarity of Britain, Norway and Sweden in providing compulsory coverage of the entire population and equal benefits, see Seierstad, 1974, p. 83-4.

12 For an interesting debate on the respective claims of Liberals and Social Democrats as social welfare innovators in Sweden, see Verney, 1972, pp. 42-59 and Haskel, 1972, pp. 306-10. Stein Kuhnle points out that Sweden was the first country in the world to introduce 'a social insurance programme that was compulsory for virtually the entire population'. Enacted in 1913, the

programme covered old age and invalidity insurance. However, although this constitutes evidence for the innovatory policy-making stance of the Liberals, Kuhnle argues that an important contributory factor was the strength of the political component of the labour movement in the *Riksdag* (27.8 per cent of parliamentary representation). See Kuhnle, 1976, pp. 1-40.

13 A recent source cites the Swedish LO as having a membership of 98 per cent of the nation's industrial and lower white-collar workers in 1974; see Hancock, 'Sweden's Emerging "Labour Socialism"' to be published in Brown (ed.), *The European Left Confronts Modernity*. Harry Eckstein suggests that 90 per cent of Norway's industrial workers are unionised compared with 50 per cent in Britain (Harry Eckstein, 1966, p. 105). A Danish official source suggests that '[the] degree of organisation in most trades affiliated to the national centre is 95-100 per cent, the chief exceptions to this rule being shop and office workers, farm workers, and domestic workers' *Denmark: An Official Handbook*, 1970, p. 187.

14 It should be made clear that the Swedish Low Income Committee was directly sponsored by the government with the objective of providing adequate statistical information on which to base policy initiatives in the welfare field. Similar considerations also applied to a later Norwegian study of the level-of-living (NOU, 1976, p. 28). Hugh Heclo, in a comparison of social welfare politics in Britain and Sweden, has suggested that policy making in Sweden has frequently been more productive because it has involved a greater degree of 'political learning' from past experience and contemporary data gathered for the purpose in hand. British politicians start from the assumption of divergent interests, whereas Swedish politicians start from the assumption that they need more information. See Heclo, 1974, pp. 304-22. The Swedish style of policy making, of which the Low Income Committee was but one manifestation, is also that which is typical of the other Scandinavian nations.

15 That such studies involve a description of social and economic inequalities makes them intrinsically controversial. The Swedish Low Income Committee was wound-up before it could issue a final report, since its findings in some areas showed a rather lesser degree of income equality than was consistent with the Social Democratic self-image. It should be mentioned, in fairness, that the Party went in the next election with the slogan 'Ökad Jämliket' – More Equality. The directives for the Norwegian study stated explicitly that the researchers must not make political recommendations. However, it was also stated that '[in] describing the situation on each indicator, deviation from equality is to be stressed' (Ringen, 1974, p. 191).

16 One useful, though by now rather dated, source for such comparisons is the United Nations publication *Incomes in Post-War Europe: A Study of Policies, Growth and Distribution*, 1967.

17 A study of taxes and transfers in Sweden demonstrated that, for groups with short working time and with incomes below the lowest income bracket, disposable income was appreciably higher than taxable income (Söderström, 1971). The results of this study are reported in Lindbeck, 1975. I have used this latter source extensively in arriving at my conclusions, since it provides an excellent summary of much of the Swedish research on income distribution prior to 1974.

18 The discussion of political resources has led to the emergence of the concept of 'political poverty', which covers all those social and economic impediments which make it difficult for the deprived to exercise their formal political rights. This subject is touched on briefly by Uusitalo. Willy Martinussen has made a major empirical study of barriers to participation in Norway, and has shown

that economic means, social opportunities, intellectual background and mental and physical health are all highly related to the degree of 'political poverty'. However, in terms of a comparison between Scandinavia and other advanced nations, it is important to note that organisational membership is found to be a factor facilitating greater participation. Although Martinussen does not himself make this point, this suggests that the degree of 'political poverty' may be somewhat less in Scandinavia than elsewhere, since, as was noted in Chapter 1, one of its distinguishing characteristics is the high degree of organisation, and, in particular, working-class organisation. See Martinussen, 1977.

19 I say 'fairly accurate' simply because we do not have adequate evidence of the *underlying* beliefs of any political groups. Usually, the most that is possible is to infer beliefs from actions, and it then becomes tautological to 'explain' those actions by the beliefs thus inferred. This problem is inherent in all studies of the relationship between beliefs and action, and I would not wish to excoriate a fault in others, which will also be manifested in the analysis which follows. However, I would like to emphasise that my conclusions are tentative. I will present some survey findings of non-socialist elite beliefs in Scandinavia, but this type of research is also suspect to the degree that it measures only the image that individuals wish to have presented to the world. It is perhaps significant, however, that the image that Scandinavian non-socialist elites wish to present to the world is distinctly egalitarian.

20 For a discussion of the concept of an 'image of society' see Castles, 1974, pp. 289-98.

Chapter 3 Paradoxes of Scandinavian political development

1 The capitalisation of Bourgeois is intended to emphasise the distinction from the 'bourgeois' parties. The whole paradox of Scandinavian political development can be summarised by pointing to the fact that the bourgeois parties do not have a distinctly Bourgeois image of society.

2 The 1956 and 1968 surveys of class and party preference reported by Arend Lijphart both show the advantage of the religious parties combined over the Labour Party amongst working-class voters. The recent growth in electoral support for the Labour Party makes it seem probable that this anomaly of Dutch politics has ceased to be operative.

3 An excellent critical review of the literature on working-class deference is to be found in Kavanagh, 1971.

4 It should be noted that Uusitalo's category of entrepreneurs seems to include the self-employed. This would explain the implicit conflict between Valen and Rokkan's finding and the data in Table 3.2 concerning Norwegian entrepreneurs' propensity to vote for the Labour Party. Similar caution is necessary in interpreting the Swedish data in Table 3.2.

5 The largely peasant-based parties of democratisation in Norway and Denmark were not called Liberal parties, but *Venstre* — literally Left parties — to contrast with their opponents, *Höyre* (*Hojre* in Denmark and *Högern* in Sweden) — literally Right parties. That the comparable party in Swedish was called a Liberal party is a reflection of the fact that it was founded at a rather later date than the Norwegian or Danish parties.

6 The terms 'strike volume' and 'strike participation', as well as my statements regarding the magnitude of strike activity, are based on the excellent paper 'Long-run Trends in Strike Activity in Comparative Perspective' by Douglas A. Hibbs, Jr. of the Department of Political Science at the Massachussetts

Institute of Technology. It will be evident that my discussion of strike activity owes a great deal to Dr. Hibbs's analysis and I would like to acknowledge his kind permission to allow me to quote his findings prior to their publication elsewhere.

7 The extent of industrial unrest in Scandinavia before 1930 is probably not widely known among non-Scandinavian specialists. However, ignorance in this respect can lead to curious inversions of historical causality. Discussing the reasons for the Scandinavian Social Democrats' pre-war political success, Paterson and Campbell suggest that the parties 'evidently benefited from their close association with the trade unions in a part of the world characterised by a low degree of industrial unrest' Paterson and Campbell, 1974, p. 9. The point is that Scandinavia was only characterised by a low degree of industrial unrest *after* the Social Democrats had achieved political office.

8 The reported correlation between change in Socialist/Labour political power (interwar to postwar change in average percentage of cabinet posts held) and change in public sector allocation (change in nondefence general government expenditure as a percentage of GNP, 1938-72) is +0.823. The correlation between change in public sector allocation and change in strike volume (interwar to postwar change in average man-days lost per 1,000 employees) is −0.812.

9 In the Netherlands, the weakness of the party of the Right, the fragmentation of the religious parties (which prevented an alternative coalescence of the Right wing in any one of them) and the strength of the working class within the religious parties (and, particularly, the Catholic party) seems to have offered a similar guarantee. The agreement-to-disagree rule, argued by Lijphart to have been a fundamental premise of the politics of accommodation, ensured that the gains resulting from a co-operative strategy would not be distributed in a completely one-sided manner. Thus:

> On issues considered vital by any bloc, no decision can be made without either their concurrence or at least substantial concessions to them. The veto power is not absolute. No single group can block action completely, but its wishes will be considered seriously and accommodated as much as possible by the others. In short, the rule is majoritarianism tempered by the spirit of concurrent majority (Lijphart, 1968b, p. 125).

In the context of the theoretical argument I am advancing, it must be stressed that the guarantee offered the working class that a co-operative strategy will not be subverted to their disadvantage is the balance of political and social forces, of which the agreement-to-disagree rule is but an expression.

10 A rather more plausible explanation of the immediate events leading to the emergence of absolutist rule was that it came into being as a consequence of the direct pressure exerted by the increasingly influential merchant class which was utterly disgusted by the aristocratic mismanagement which, in its view, had lost Scania to the Swedes. The monarchy remained the creature of the merchants to a considerable extent − fostering trade and industry in the eighteenth century − and in 1848 could not resist their demands which were backed up by peasant discontent.

11 Just the same purpose, indeed, as is served by the admission of a small degree of cultural indeterminacy by those proponents of the 'general laws of capitalist development' who are more interested in the elaboration of general laws than in understanding the nature of capitalist development.

12 On the role of the peasantry, see Østerud, 1974. On differences in industrial development, see Lafferty, 1971 and Kuhnle, 1975.

13 See, in particular, Barrington Moore, Jr., 1966, Immanuel Wallerstein, 1974 and Perry Anderson, 1974. It is interesting that each of these writers has great difficulties in fitting Scandinavia into his own theoretical framework. Moore suggests that 'the peasants have become part of democratic systems by taking up fairly specialized forms of commercial farming' (p. 422), when, in fact, only in Denmark did wide-scale commercial farming precede substantial peasant incorporation. Wallerstein argues that Sweden is a 'mild deviant case' [sic] in having strong state machinery in the model of the core states of western Europe not because of its economic strength, but rather because 'agriculture was weak, and its aristocrats wished to take hold of the profits of other lands for want of being able to create them on their own' (p. 312). To Anderson, Sweden seems to contradict the normal canons of Marxist explanation. Thus, he argues, '[the] historical underdetermination of Swedish Absolutism was never more visible than in [its] strange climax. A facultative State finished in apparently full contingency' (p. 191). Since 'facultative' means optional, one presumes that the tautology is designed to emphasise the distinctiveness of Swedish political development. For a treatment which argues that Moore's mistake, in respect of Sweden at least, is an underestimation of the role of the independent peasantry, see Castles, 1973, pp. 313-31.

14 Østerud is amongst the scholars who stress the dissimilarities of the development of the Scandinavian agrarian structures. Thus he suggests that, whilst the Scandinavian political systems have become quite similar, 'their historical and agrarian preconditions are remarkably different' (Østerud, 1974, p. 6). However, it is fascinating that in making a contrast with Britain, it is the similarities which are emphasised.

15 Comparisons between Britain and Scandinavia are frequently made (presumably because both became democracies), but less frequently between Scandinavia and Prussia. This is strange because in terms of low urbanisation, high literacy, weakness of liberalism, early welfare legislation and, of course, early strength of Social Democracy, there are remarkable similarities. Clearly, in light of the argument presented here, the difference is in the relative positions of the peasants (largely independent freeholders in Scandinavia and landless in Prussia) and the upper classes (largely urban in Scandinavia and rural in Prussia).

16 This quotation is from Pär-Erik Back, 1967, pp.28-9. It is cited by Christopher Wheeler, 1975, p. 167. I would like to record that some of the ideas expressed in these last few paragraphs owe much to long discussions with Chris Wheeler.

17 This latter accords with Kuhnle's view: 'The different agrarian structures created dissimilar systems of status inequalities, and one of our hypotheses should be that the Norwegian structure made for the development of more egalitarian values and a weaker support for individualist-success ideology' (Kuhnle, 1976, pp. 31-2).

References

ADLER-KARLSSON, GUNNAR (1967), *Functional Socialism: A Swedish Theory for Democratic Socialization*, Stockholm, Bokförlaget Prisma.

ANDERSON, PERRY (1961), 'Sweden: Mr Crosland's Dreamland', *New Left Review*, no. 7.

ANDERSON, PERRY (1974), *Lineages of the Absolutist State*, London, New Left Books.

ANDREN, NILS (1961), *Modern Swedish Government*, Stockholm, Almqvist & Wiksell.

BACK, PÄR-ERIK (1967), *Sammanslutningarnas roll i politiken 1870-1910*, Lund, Studentlitteratur.

BEER, SAMUEL (1965), *Modern British Politics*, London, Faber & Faber.

BORRE, OLE (1974), 'Denmark's Protest Election of December 1973', *Scandinavian Political Studies*, vol. 9.

BUTLER, DAVID and STOKES, DONALD (1969), *Political Change in Britain*, London, Macmillan.

CARLSSON, STEN (1962), *Bonde-präst-ämbetsman*, Stockholm, Bokförlaget Prisma.

CARROLL, LEWIS (1865), *Alice's Adventures in Wonderland*, London, Macmillan.

CASTLES, F. G. (1973), 'Barrington Moore's Thesis and Swedish Political Development', *Government and Opposition, vol. 8, no. 3.*
Political Studies, vol. xxii, no. 3.

CASTLES, F. G. (1977), 'Scandinavia: The Politics of Stability', in Roy Macridis (ed.), *Modern Political Systems: Europe*, Prentice-Hall.

CHILDS, MARQUIS (1936), *Sweden: The Middle Way*, New Haven, Conn., Yale University Press.

CROSLAND, C. A. R. (1956), *The Future of Socialism*, London, Jonathan Cape.

CUTRIGHT, PHILLIPS (1965), 'Political Structure, Economic Development and National Social Security Programs', *American Journal of Sociology.*

DAHRENDORF, RALF (1967), *Society and Democracy in Germany*, London, Weidenfeld & Nicolson.

DAMGAARD, E. (1974), 'Stability and Change in the Danish Party System over Half a Century', *Scandinavian Political Studies*, vol. 9.

DENMARK: AN OFFICIAL HANDBOOK (1970), Copenhagen, Ministry of Foreign Affairs.

DERRY, T. K. (1973), *A History of Modern Norway 1814-1972*, Oxford, Clarendon Press.

DUVERGER, MAURICE (1960), 'La Sociologie des Partis Politiqués', in G. Gurvitch (ed.), *Traité de Sociologie*, Paris, Presses Universitaires, vol. II.

ECKSTEIN, HARRY (1966), *Division and Cohesion in Democracy*, Princeton, New Jersey, Princeton University Press.

ELVANDER, NILS (1974), 'Collective Bargaining and Incomes Policy in the Nordic Countries', *British Journal of Industrial Relations*, vol. XII.

ELVANDER, NILS (1977), *Scandinavian Social Democracy: Present Trends and Future Prospects*, Berlin, European Consortium for Political Research.

ERICHSEN, EIVIND (1976), *Some Aspects of Economic Planning in Norway Today*, Oslo, Norway Information.

FLORA, PETER (1973), 'Historical Processes of Social Mobilization: Urbanization and Literacy 1850-1965', in S. N. Eisenstadt and Stein Rokkan, (eds), *Building States and Nations*, vol. 1, Beverly Hills, Sage Publications.

FORSEBÄCK, LENNART (1976), *Industrial Relations and Employment in Sweden*, Stockholm, The Swedish Institute.

GALENSON, WALTER (1968), 'Scandinavia' in Walter Galenson (ed.), *Comparative Labour Movements*, New York, Russell & Russell.

GALENSON, WALTER (1970), *Labor in Norway*, New York, Russell & Russell.

GALTUNG, JOHAN and TORD HØIVIK (1968), *On the Definition and Theory of Development with a View to the Application of Rank Order Indicators in the Elaboration of a Composite Index of Human Resources*, Paris, UNESCO, COM/WS/68.

GESSER, B. and E. FASTH (1973), *Gymnasiebildning och social skiktning*, Stockholm, Utbildningsförlaget.

GRUCHY, A. G. (1966), *Comparative Economic Systems*, Boston, Houghton Mifflin.

HANCOCK, M. DONALD (1972), *Sweden: The Politics of Postindustrial Change*, Hinsdale, Illinois, Druden Press.

HANCOCK, M. DONALD (1976), 'Elite Images and System Change in Sweden', in L. N. Lindberg (ed.), *The Future of Industrial Society*, New York, David McKay.

HANCOCK, M. DONALD (1977), 'Sweden's Emerging "Labor Socialism"', in B. E. Brown (ed.), *The European Left Confronts Modernity*. New York, Cyrco Press.

HASKEL, BARBARA G. (1972), 'What is Innovation? Sweden's Liberals, Social Democrats and Political Creativity', *Political Studies*, vol. xx, no. 3.

HASKEL, BARBARA G. (1976), *The Scandinavian Option*, Oslo, Universitetsforlaget.

HECKSCHER, GUNNAR (1948), 'Pluralist Democracy', *Social Research*, No. 15.

HECLO, HUGH (1974), *Modern Social Politics in Britain and Sweden*, New Haven, Yale University Press.

HEIDENHEIMER, A. J. and F. C. LANDON (1968), *Business Associations and the Financing of Political Parties*, The Hague, Martinus Nijhoff.

HEIDAR, KNUT (1977), 'The Norwegian Labour Party', in W. E. Paterson and

A. H. Thomas (eds), *Social Democratic Parties in Western Europe*, London, Croom Helm.

HEISLER, MARTIN (1974), 'Institutionalizing Societal Cleavages in a Cooptive Polity: The Growing Importance of the Output Side in Belgium', in Martin Heilser (ed.), *Politics in Europe*, New York, David McKay.

HIBBS, DOUGLAS A. (1976), 'Long-run Trends in Strike Activity in Comparative Perspective', Massachussetts Institute of Technology.

HIGLEY, JOHN *et al.* (1976), *Elite Structure and Ideology*, Oslo, Universitetsforlaget.

HILL, KEITH (1974), 'Political Change in a Segmented Society', in Richard Rose (ed.), *Electoral Behaviour: A Comparative Handbook*, London, Collier Macmillan.

HOLMBERG, PER (1970), *Svenska folkets inkomster*, Stockholm, SOU, no. 34.

HOVDE, B. J. (1943), *The Scandinavian Countries, 1720-1865: The Rise of the Middle Classes*, vol. II, Boston, Chapman & Grimes.

ILO (1972), *The Cost of Social Security, 1964-6*, Geneva.

INGHAM, G. K. (1974), *Strikes and Industrial Conflict: Britain and Scandinavia*, London, Macmillan.

JENKINS, DAVID (1968), *Sweden: The Progress Machine*, London, Robert Hale.

JOHANSSON, STEN (1971), *Om levnadsnivåundersökningen*, Stockholm, Allmänna Förlaget.

JOHANSSON, STEN (1973), 'The Level of Living Survey: A Presentation', *Acta Sociologica*, 16(3).

KAIM-CAUDLE, P. R. (1973), *Comparative Social Policy and Social Security*, London, Martin Robertson.

KAVANAGH, DENNIS (1971), 'The Deferential English: A Comparative Critique', *Government and Opposition*, vol. 6, no. 3.

KELLER, SUZANNE (1963), *Beyond the Ruling Class*, New York, Random House.

KORNHAUSER, WILLIAM (1959), *The Politics of Mass Society*, Chicago, The Free Press.

KUHLMANN, STIG (1974), *Danish Labour Market Conditions 1974*, Copenhagen, Ministry of Labour.

KUHNLE, STEIN (1975), *Patterns of Social and Political Mobilization: a Historical Analysis of the Nordic Countries*, London, Sage Publications.

KUHNLE, STEIN (1976), 'Political and socio-economic conditions for the early development of social policy legislation: a comparison of Denmark, Norway and Sweden', Louvain, *European Consortium for Political Research*.

KUZNETS, SIMON (1960), 'Economic Growth of Small Nations', in Austin Robinson (ed.), *The Economic Consequences of the Size of Nations*, London, Macmillan.

KUZNETS, SIMON (1971), *Economic Growth of Nations: Total Output and Production Structure*, Cambridge, Mass, Harvard University Press.

KVAVIK, R. B. (1976), *Interest Groups in Norwegian Politics*, Oslo, Universitetsforlaget.

LAFFERTY, WILLIAM M. (1971), *Economic Development and the Response of Labor in Scandinavia*, Oslo, Universitetsforlaget.

LANDAUER, CARL (1959), *European Socialism: A History of Ideas and Movements*, Vols I & II, Berkeley, University of California Press.

LAURING, PALLE (1968), *A History of the Kingdom of Denmark*, Copenhagen, Høst & Søn.

LAUX, W. E. (1963), *Interest Groups in Danish Politics*, Ann Arbor, University Microfilms.

LENSKI, G. (1966), *Power and Privilege*, New York, McGraw-Hill.

LIJPHART, AREND (1968a), 'Consociational Democracy', *World Politics*, vol. XXI.

LIJPHART, AREND (1968b), *The Politics of Accommodation*, Berkeley, University of California Press.

LINDBECK, ASSAR (1975), 'Inequality and Redistribution Policy Issues (Principles and Swedish Experience)', in OECD, *Education, Inequality and Life Chances*, vol. 2, Paris, OECD.

LIPSET, S. M. (1963), *Political Man*, New York, Doubleday & Co, Anchor Books.

LIPSET, S. M. and STEIN ROKKAN (1967), *Party Systems and Voter Alignments*, New York, The Free Press.

McCLELLAN, DAVID (1975), *Marx*, London, Fontana.

McKENZIE, ROBERT and ALLAN SILVER (1968), *Angels in Marble*, London, Heinemann.

MACKIE, T. T. and R. ROSE (1974), *The International Almanac of Electoral History*, London, Macmillan.

MARSHALL, T. H. (1950), *Citizenship and Social Class*, Cambridge University Press.

MARTINUSSEN, WILLY (1977), *The Distant Democracy*, London, John Wiley & Sons.

MARX, KARL (1852), 'The Chartists', *New York Daily Tribune*, 25 August.

MILL, J. S. (1967), *A System of Logic*, London, Longmans.

MILLER, K. E. (1968), *Government and Politics in Denmark*, Boston, Houghton Mifflin.

MOE, FINN (1937), *Does Norwegian Labor Seek the Middle Way?*, New York, The League for Industrial Democracy.

MOORE, BARRINGTON,JR. (1966), *Social Origins of Dictatorship and Democracy*, Boston, Beacon Press.

MUKHERJE, SANTOSH (1972), *Making Labour Markets Work*, London, PEP Broadsheet, no. 532.

MYRDAL, ALVA (1971), *Towards Equality*, Stockholm, Bokförlaget Prisma.

NIELSEN, H. J. (1976), 'The Uncivic Culture: Attitudes towards the Political System in Denmark, and Vote for the Progress Party 1973-1975', *Scandinavian Political Studies*.

NOU (1976), *Levekärdundersøkelsen*, no. 28.

OECD (1974), *Manpower Policy in Denmark*, Paris.

OECD (1974), *The Educational Situation in OECD Countries*, Paris.

OECD (1977), *Economic Survey: Norway*, Paris.

ÖHMAN, BERNDT (1974), *LO and Labour Market Policy since the Second World War*, Stockholm, Bokförlaget Prisma.

OLSON, MANCUR, JR. (1963), 'Rapid Growth as a Destabilizing Force', *The Journal of Economic History*, vol. XXIII, no. 4.

ØSTERUD, ØYVIND (1974), *Agrarian Structure and Peasant Politics in Scandinavia*, Unpublished PhD thesis, London School of Economics.

PARKIN, FRANK (1967), 'Working Class Conservatives: A Theory of Political Deviance', *British Journal of Sociology*, vol. 18.

PARKIN, FRANK (1971), *Class Inequality and Political Order*, London, MacGibbon & Kee.

PATERSON, W. E. and IAN CAMPBELL (1974), *Social Democracy in Post-War Europe*, London, Macmillan.

PESONEN, PERTTI (1974), 'Finland: Party Support in a Fragmented System', in R. Rose (ed.), *Electoral Behaviour: A Comparative Handbook*, New York, The Free Press.

RINGEN, STEIN (1966), 'Welfare Studies in Scandinavia', *Scandinavian Political Studies*, vol. 9.

ROKKAN, STEIN (1966), 'Norway: Numerical Democracy and Corporate Pluralism', in R. A Dahl (ed.), *Political Oppositions in Western Democracies*, New Haven, Conn., Yale University Press.

ROKKAN, STEIN (1970), *Citizens, Elections, Parties*, Oslo, Universitetsforlaget.

ROSE, RICHARD (ed.) (1974), *Electoral Behaviour: A Comparative Handbook*, New York, The Free Press.

ROSS, A. M. and HARTMAN, P. T. (1960), *Changing Patterns of Industrial Conflict*, New York, John Wiley & Sons.

RUIN, OLOF (1974), Participatory Democracy and Corporativism: The Case of Sweden', *Scandinavian Political Studies*, vol. 9.

RUSSETT, BRUCE M., *et al.* (1964), *World Handbook of Political and Social Indicators*, New Haven, Conn., Yale University Press.

RUSTOW, D. A. (1956), 'Scandinavian Working Multiparty Systems', in S. Neumann (ed.), *Modern Political Parties*, University of Chicago Press.

SAMUELSSON, KURT (1968), *From Great Power to Welfare State*, London, Allen & Unwin.

SARTORI, GIOVANNI (1970), 'Concept misformation in comparative politics', *American Political Science Review*, vol. 54.

SARTORI, GIOVANNI (1976), *Parties and party systems*, Cambridge University Press.

SAUERBERG, STEEN (1976), 'The Uncivic Culture: Communication and the Political System in Denmark 1973-1975', *Scandinavian Political Studies*, vol. 11.

SCASE, RICHARD (1976), 'Images of Progress, 1: Sweden', *New Society*, 23-30 December.

SCASE, RICHARD (1977), *Social Democracy in Capitalist Society*, London, Croom Helm.

SEIERSTAD, S. (1974), 'The Norwegian Economy', in Natalie R. Ramsøy (ed.), *Norwegian Society*, Oslo, Universitetsforlaget.

SJÖMAN, VILGOT (1968), *I am Curious (Yellow)*, New York, Grove Press.

SÖDERPALM, S. A. (1975), 'The Crisis Agreement and the Social Democratic Road to Power', in Steven Koblik (ed.), *Sweden's Development from Poverty to Affluence*, Minneapolis, University of Minnesota Press.

SÖDERSTRÖM, L. (1971), *Den svenska köpkraftsfördelningen 1967*, Stockholm, SOU, no. 39.

SVENSSON, PALLE (1974), 'Support for the Danish Social Democratic Party 1924-39 – Growth and Response', *Scandinavian Political Studies*, vol. 9.

THOMAS, ALASTAIR (1977), 'Social Democracy in Denmark', in W. E. Paterson and A. H. Thomas (eds), *Social Democratic Parties in Western Europe*, London, Croom Helm.

TILTON, T. A. (1974), 'The Social Origins of Liberal Democracy: The Swedish Case', *American Political Science Review*.

TINGSTEN, H. (1973), *The Swedish Social Democrats*, New Jersey, The Bedminster Press.

TORGERSEN, ULF (1970), 'The Trend toward Political Consensus: The Case of Norway', in E. Allardt and Stein Rokkan (eds), *Mass Politics*, New York, The Free Press.

TORGERSEN, ULF (1974), 'Political Institutions', in Natalie R. Ramsøy, *Norwegian Society*, Oslo, Universitetsforlaget.

UNESCO Statistical Yearbook 1975 (1976), Paris.

US Arms Control and Disarmament Agency (1972), *World Military Expenditures, 1971*, Washington.

UUSITALO, HANNU (1975a), *Income and Welfare: A Study of Income as a Component of Welfare in the Scandinavian Countries in the 1970s*, Helsinki, Research Group for Comparative Sociology.

UUSITALO, HANNU (1975b), *Class Structure and Party Choice*, Helsinki, Research Group for Comparative Sociology.

VALEN, HENRY and DANIEL KATZ (1964), *Political Parties in Norway*, Oslo, Universitetsforlaget.

VALEN, HENRY and STEIN ROKKAN (1974), 'Conflict Structure and Mass Politics in a European Periphery', in R. Rose (ed.), *Electoral Behaviour: A Comparative Handbook*, New York, The Free Press.

VERNEY, DOUGLAS (1957), *Parliamentary Reform in Sweden, 1866-1921*, Oxford University Press.

VERNEY, DOUGLAS (1972), 'The Foundations of Modern Sweden: The Swift Rise and Fall of Swedish Liberalism', *Political Studies*, vol. xx, no. 1.

WALLERSTEIN, IMMANUEL (1974), *The Modern World-System*, New York, Academic Press.

WALTON, R. E. and R. B. McKERSIE (1965), *A Behavioral Theory of Labor Negotiations: An Analysis of a Social Interaction System*, New York, McGraw Hill.

WHEELER, CHRISTOPHER (1975), *White-Collar Power*, Urbana, University of Illinois Press.

WILENSKY, HAROLD (1975), *The Welfare State and Equality*, Berkeley, University of California Press.

WORRE, TORBEN (1977), 'The Decline of Danish Social Democracy', Berlin, *European Consortium for Political Research*.

Yearbook of Nordic Statistics 1975 (1976), Copenhagen and Stockholm, Nordic Council.

Index

SPRING 1984
WINTER 1985

Stanford University Libraries

3 6105 003 212 623

DATE DUE		
MAY 25 1987		
JUN 23 1987		
JUN 23 1989		

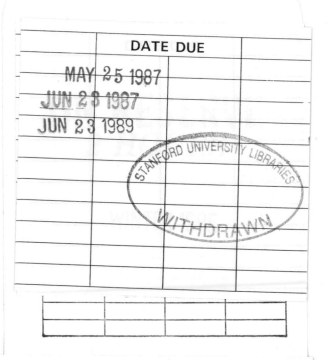

STANFORD UNIVERSITY LIBRARIES
WITHDRAWN

STANFORD UNIVERSITY LIBRARIES
STANFORD, CALIFORNIA 94305